THE IRISH DONKEY

Averil Swinfen

THE LILLIPUT PRESS
DUBLIN

Enlarged edition published 2004 by
THE LILLIPUT PRESS
62–63 Sitric Road, Arbour Hill,
Dublin 7, Ireland
www.lilliputpress.ie

Revised edition published 1975 by
J.A. ALLEN
1 Lower Grosvenor Place
Buckingham Palace Road
London

First published 1969 by
THE MERCIER PRESS
4 Bridge Street,
Cork, Ireland

A CIP record for this title is available from
The British Library.

ISBN 1 84351 042 1

Set in 12 pt on 16 pt Sabon
Printed by ßetaprint

Contents

II. THE DONKEY IN THE WORLD

Illustrations between pages 108 and 109

Foreword

I AM HONOURED to be the first person allowed to read the manuscript of this book, *The Irish Donkey*, by Averil Swinfen whom I have known for many years. A lover of animals, she has been keenly interested in them all her life. In the past, when neighbours in County Cork, we shared a mutual love of, and interest in, horses. Indeed when I decided to set up as a trainer she was, though not one of the luckiest, one of the first owners to send me a horse, and she was an enthusiastic supporter in those early days. Though the course of her life led to England for some years, it was inevitable that on her return home to Ireland, her children by then grown up, she would once again interest herself in animals. This time the animal to which she chose to devote her experience and talent was the donkey.

Donkeys are so much part of the Irish landscape and tradition that they have been too much taken for granted. With the development of better means of transport, and consequent decline of their use as beasts of burden, they could easily become extinct. They have been regarded so much as a poor relation of the horse that nobody here seems to have taken the trouble to make a study of them or supply instruction and information.

Lady Swinfen's feeling for animals alone qualifies her to write a book about them. She has had the interest and enthusiasm to do a tremendous amount of research into the history of donkeys; she has had the practical experience gained from her breeding establishment to write the sections on the care and management of donkeys; and she has the great love of donkeys which makes her such an ardent and promi-nent campaigner to get their conditions bettered and their worth recognized. She shows that they are won-derful pets, less expensive and more houseable than horses, and who can deny that many of our great horsemen, on the flat and over jumps, and in the hunting field, gained their early knowledge of riding astride a donkey?

Although the association between man and the working-type horse is nearly over, interest in the sporting and recreational spheres is as great as ever. Averil Swinfen, with the production of her book, fills a gap in Irish literature about this most neglected member of the equine family.

Vincent O'Brien

Preface & Acknowledgments to the Lilliput Edition

AFTER CLOSING the Donkey Stud in the mid-eighties, and moving house elsewhere, more than once, I had to board out my remaining animals. I would now like to thank many friends for assistance at that time. Also, much gratitude is due to all those persons in various places who helped in many ways over the years to care for my unique and much valued Twinnies, Ome and Omi (see Chapter Two).

In this edition, each chapter has had minor revisions and corrections, and Chapters One, Two, Three, Six and Nine have been substantially reworked to incorporate new material. Chapter Twenty is entirely new. Thus, some anachronisms may appear in the sections that have not been significantly changed. While I was updating this book, I received help from the following people, in addition to those mentioned in the Preface and Acknowledgments to the 1969 edition.

Father Ignatius Fennessy, OFM, the Franciscan Librarian in Killiney, furnished me with much information from his authoritative research. I am most grateful to him for his kindness. My thanks also to Seamus and Caroline Corballis for added and helpful material.

Chiefly I owe a more personal debt to Dr Tony Sweeney, a long-time friend, whose unfailing assistance has been immediately available at all times— many, many thanks for invaluable contributions.

Also I have to thank my efficient editor, Jennifer Smith, whose help and advice has been so important in the preparation of this edition. To Gillian Somerville-Large, my grateful appreciation for her generous co-operation, not only for typing these pages, but giving me much aid in checking and assembling them.

It was a joy to learn of a recent distinction accorded Vincent O'Brien, who so kindly wrote the foreword to the first edition. Ten years into his retirement, the memory of his achievements still burns brightly, as was shown when he headed the readers' poll conducted by *The Racing Post* to choose the top hundred turf celebrities.

As for my late husband, Carol, his steadfast support was always my mainstay in this highly unusual adventure.

Averil Swinfen
County Kilkenny, Ireland, 2004

Preface & Acknowledgments to the 1969 Edition

I THINK THAT IF, before I had started this book, I had read the suggestion made by Rev. J.P. Mahaffy, DD CVO, that to write a monograph about the ass one 'must not only be a zoologist, but a historian, and also even a psychologist', I would never have dared to put pen to paper, having absolutely no pretensions to any of these accomplishments. Indeed, I have nothing to excuse me at all, save a deep affection and respect for these animals and better opportunities than most people to observe them, and the hope that anything that tends to increase interest in and regard for them will equally tend to reduce the indignities and suffering to which they have for so long been subject.

Not that they have been entirely without protectors. The Irish Society for the Prevention of Cruelty to Animals has done, and continues to do, magnificent work for the donkey, no less than for other animals, and no praise is too great for it.

I am only too conscious that there are many matters of great interest concerning asses that I have omitted, some because they have been more than adequately dealt with by previous writers, and others because they require a technical knowledge that I do not possess.

The broken-coloured breeding theory put forward in this book is my own untutored idea and if those more learned than I should be sufficiently interested to investigate further, it would indeed be of great interest to us donkey lovers.

In Ireland the older word 'ass' is used throughout the countryside in preference to the word 'donkey'. This latter word used to be pronounced to rhyme with 'monkey'. It is derived from the word 'dun' meaning a brownish-coloured horse; the suffix k-ey is a double diminutive, making it a little little horse. It seems to have been a late eighteenth-century Celtic and English word. In my writing I have not kept to either word, using each indiscriminately as it came to mind. The term 'broken-coloured' I have used to incorporate piebald, skewbald and any other decisively marked ass of two or more colours.

Though County Clare is now my home and holds my heart, as it has that of others of us in past generations who have been connected with it, the happy memories of childhood, however, never allow me to forget the county of Cork, one of the loveliest counties in Ireland and the home of my family for generations.

So many people have been kind enough to show interest and give assistance towards putting this book together that it is impossible to thank them all individually. Some have given generously of their time and skill in unearthing for me information that I had difficulty in finding, others very kindly wrote to me volunteering notes, tales and pieces of information: all showed boundless goodwill. I can but assure them collectively of my gratitude.

There are some, however, whose help was quite invaluable and to them I tender my sincere thanks: Desmond J. Clarke, MA FLAI, Librarian of the Royal Dublin Society; Alan R. Eager, FLAI, Assistant Librarian of the Royal Dublin Society; Michael Flanagan, FLAI, Librarian of the Clare County Library, Ennis, and his assistants; Dr J.S. Jackson, Keeper of the Natural History Division of the National Museum of Ireland; and Dr Thomas Wall of the Irish Folklore Commission.

I am indebted to the staff of the Royal Irish Academy and of The National Library, Dublin, and Miss Hynes of The Sweeney Memorial Library, Kilkee, County Clare, for their assistance; Mrs Maureen Kenny, BA, of Kenny's Bookshop, Galway, for her constant help and encouragement; Mrs Sonia Kelly for kind assistance in typing and stringing together my earlier notes; Morgan O'Loughlin, MVB MRCVS, for reading and giving me his valued advice on Chapter Nine ('Care').

My thanks are also due to *Life Magazine* and *Ireland's Own* for so kindly giving me permission to include in this book excerpts from their publications.

When we started our stud here, we were unaware of the existence of any other donkey breeders and we have always been sincerely grateful for all that has been done to help us by our local vets. Their professional etiquette requires that I should not name them but, even though they remain anonymous, I wish to thank them wholeheartedly.

I am grateful too to our donkey girls and the members of our establishment for their understanding and willing assistance in freeing me to pursue my donkey lore.

I greatly appreciate the kind assistance I have received from Countess von der Schulenburg, in the work she has done and the care she has taken over the final manuscript.

As for my husband, his unfailing encouragement and help have been my main support along the devious pathways of the donkey trail which we have travelled together.

Finally, I would like to thank our many 'donkey friends' in County Clare and elsewhere for much encouragement, help and genuine interest shown in our stud adventurings, hoping that we can continue to further the interests of the donkey with the same happiness and gaiety.

Averil Swinfen
County Clare, Ireland, 1969

Introduction

THERE HAVE BEEN MANY changes in the life of the Irish donkey since this book was first published in 1969 and reissued in 1975. In those not-so-distant days the donkey was still an integral part of the Irish rural scene. Now it has almost disappeared. For while there are a number of them kept as pets, the donkey as a working animal is seldom seen, except occasionally in remote rural areas—no more carting milk-churns to the creamery, toiling on the turf bogs, hauling seaweed from the seashore, and divers other labours, since today mechanization has taken over these tasks.

The intervening years have not all been happy ones for our long-eared friends. Those kept as pets are well nurtured and many have developed into splendid animals. Others have experienced the disregard too often meted out to creatures that lack commercial value and have suffered neglect and cruelty. However, since the advent of donkey sanctuaries in the country, notably at Liscarroll, County Cork, and the Richard Martin Restfields in counties Wicklow and Donegal, these sorrowful animals are rescued to be nursed with affectionate attention. Later, when recovered, some are leased out into suitable homes. Those that have fallen into the hands of callous dealers and been dispatched overseas seldom meet other than a pitiless end. There remain some fine donkeys in Ireland, but not 'going for a song' as in days gone by.

In September 1970, together with the late Mrs Murray Mitchell and other enthusiastic supporters, we founded the Irish Donkey Society (IDS) at a gathering in Limerick, having previously advertised in the press for any interested persons to join us there.

The main aims of the Society were to raise the status of the animal and to stamp out cruelty and ill treatment. Also, as more and more donkeys were participating in agricultural shows, it was to act as a governing body to which show committees could refer for the drawing up of rules and other matters, including the desired conformation points upon which the donkeys were to be judged. Happily, within two years donkeys were permitted to join the élite of our domestic animals at the renowned Royal Dublin Society Horse Show, where they continue to disport themselves with distinction.

Simultaneously in 1970, affairs moved ahead at our stud at Spanish Point, County Clare, for with the help of Bord Fáilte, our venture was officially opened as a tourist attraction by Dr Patrick Hillery, the Minister of External Affairs. It provided conducted tours of the farm, rides and trap drives for children, a snack room, and a donkey souvenir shop. Also on the programme were short safari treks into the Burren. This, combined with visiting mares for service to our various coloured stallions, led to busy times after the previous five years, which had been relatively relaxed.

A curious addition to our stud, though not born there, was Paddy Medina, a grey gelding with short extra legs, complete with hooves, attached to the inner side of both natural forelegs. These were not monstrosities, but reversions to features of early equine ancestors. Another novel acquisition was Firefly, a mule who when suspicious of any unusual activities afoot, would sit for long spells in a dog-like pose. A most treasured donkey is 34-year-old Susie, an early emigrant from our stud to my Humphreys cousins in Somerset, where she has helped to raise the family.

As our stock increased we sold some to commendable persons, both at home and abroad, always in pairs or as a companion to another animal. Those that were deemed suitable and were fittingly handled we donated to homes for handicapped children.

I found that the years ahead were monopolized by activities associated with the Irish donkey: I edited the Irish Donkey Society magazine, *Assile*; periodically contributed to its counterparts in other countries; and wrote *Donkeys Galore*.

Early in the 1980s, after family illness, bereavement,

and a subsequent move of the stud to nearby Kilfenora, it became impracticable to keep the enterprise
afloat. A sad time for all concerned, for it was unique
of its kind in Ireland. Arguably there was not another
collection of *Equus asinus* anywhere, wild or domestic, comprising the variety of colours, markings and
other characteristics of their original species as were
incorporated in our herd of more than one hundred
animals at the culmination of almost twenty years
agrowing.

Visits to donkey locations in other countries
proved most enlightening. It was a joy to see again
stock we had exported, meet their owners and other
donkey enthusiasts from as far afield as Australia,
Fiji, the USA, and other places nearer home, while
exchanging the latest donkey news.

A truly exceptional experience was a visit in 1981
to Hai Bar, the Biblical Wildlife Reserve in Israel, 40
km north of Eilat. Having arrived there alone early
one morning, I was brought by a game warden in a
small tractor-trailer to see the wild asses. Of the two
resident herds, one was of the Somali breed (*Equus
somaliensis*) and the other species an Asiatic wild ass
(*Equus onager*). These handsome animals, while living in close proximity, remain in separate herds; the
mares, guarded by their stallions, breed only among
their own species. I was permitted to wander and
photograph close by and it was fascinating to see
their specific markings, colourings, and general for-
mation and to note which distinctive features are

inherited in our domestic Irish donkeys.

Set up by Dr Elisabeth D. Svendsen MBE, The Donkey Sanctuary, which manages the centre in Liscarroll under its director Paddy Barrett, as efficient as he is popular, incorporated the International Donkey Protection Trust. While this trust confines its splendid work to projects outside Britain and Ireland, any international communication with the Irish donkey is to be welcomed and supported.

It is difficult to assess the present number of donkeys in Ireland as they are not registered; however, the interest in those that subsist continues. And, with the constant supervision of the various sanctuaries and the Irish Society for the Prevention of Cruelty to Animals, the Irish donkey has every hope of remaining one of the most cherished of its kind.

I

THE DONKEY IN IRELAND

1. *Origins*

T HE IRISH ASS. What sort of image does that bring to mind? Certainly not that of a large, swift-footed, vari-coloured creature, and yet there is no doubt that the ancestors of our present domestic ass were so described.

The wild asses of Africa are held by some authorities to be the source of our present domestic ass, especially those that came from Nubia, Abyssinia, and other parts of North Africa east of the Nile. They are zoologically known as *Equus asinus taeniopus*, the final word being applied to them because in some of the species the lower limbs show dark stripe-like markings. (Many of our contemporary asses still produce these horizontal stripes on their legs.) Most of these asses had the dorsal stripe along the ridge of the back, continuing into the mane and tail, and also a distinct cross stripe over the shoulder, and were in colour a mouse-grey—in fact, the colour that we associate with our more ordinary domestic ass of today. The Somali wild ass, *Equus somaliensis*, which still survives under careful protection, differed from its previously described neighbour by being greyer in colour, more a stone grey, having only a slight indication of a dorsal stripe, more numerous black markings on the legs and, above all, a complete absence of the cross stripe over the shoulders.

Though these wild asses were larger and stronger looking than our average Irish ass, we can still find a good mixture of their colourings and markings amongst our present-day animals. Yet, if we assume that the African wild ass is the ancestor of our modern one, we dismiss too lightly the Asiatic wild asses, especially the onager family, *Equus onager*, *onager indicus* and *hemippus*, which roamed the plains of Asia, western India, Tibet, Afghanistan, Persia, Syria, and were even heard of as far as China.

They differed so slightly from each other that they can be described together. All being extremely fleet-footed, with smaller ears than the African wild asses, they stood between eleven and twelve hands high. Their colours were white and chestnut (brownish-yellow). The white ones occasionally had yellow blotches on their sides and neck, and the dorsal stripe was dark brown of varying breadth, with sometimes a white edge to it. The mane stood erect and the tail had short hairs at the base that grew longer and blacker towards the end, so that it appeared tufted.

The chestnut ones seem to have varied in shades with darker dorsal stripes of the same colourings, and some animals from each colour group showed a shoulder stripe and faint bars on the legs. William Ridgeway relates that in Syria these were often referred to erroneously as 'wild mules' in spite of the fact that they bred freely. Frederick Zeuner calls all the Asiatic wild asses 'half-asses' or 'hemiones' (from the Greek, hemi=half, oinos=one). All had a most strident bray. Other interesting animals included in the category of Asiatic wild asses are the kiangs of Central Asia, often called 'neither horse nor ass', looking more like a mixture of a horse and an ass than does a mule or jennet. The kiangs of Tibet and Mongolia seldom lived at an altitude lower than 10,000 feet. They stood over thirteen hands high and differed from the onagers in their colouring, which ranged from chestnut to bay (reddish-brown) and sandy fawn on the upper parts of their bodies, with off-white underparts and with a very narrow brown dorsal stripe. Their hindquarters were more developed in length and strength than those of onagers and they had different voices.

That there were wild asses in Libya in the fourth century BCE has been mentioned by Herodotus in *The Histories*, and it seems that they continued to exist there until mediaeval times. Frederick Zeuner writes that the North African wild asses (which must have included the Libyan wild asses) were last seen in the Atlas Mountains and did not survive the Roman period. These, he states, were depicted on rock pictures and Roman mosaics, but as he gives no description of them, and I have not been able to find one elsewhere, I do not know whether or not they were a different species, and if so whether they were indigenous to North Africa or just migrants. I found this description in an account of the asses used in mule breeding in the USA published by a Mr Killgore at the end of the nineteenth century:

> In the province of Catalonia in old Spain, there exists a race of asses, bred with great care for many centuries, having been introduced into that country by the Moors at the time of their conquest of that Kingdom (in the eighth century). They are black in colour, with white or mealy muzzles, and whitish or greyish bellies, varying but little in form, but greatly in size.

In present-day North Africa the majority of asses are very like our familiar mouse-coloured animal though much smaller. The larger dark brown to black animals with grey or grey flecked bellies are also present, and occasionally the light chestnut or greyish-white ones lacking the cross stripes are to be seen.

However, in describing these wild asses, it will be noticed that there is no mention of certain colours, such as black, roans and broken colours. This makes us wonder how they quite liberally made their appearance into our present-day ass family. Zoologists are unanimous in regarding their colouring and stripes as being among the principal indications that the African and Asiatic wild asses are separate breeds.

It seems fairly obvious that the descendants of these animals must have met somewhere to produce the present colours. Where and how this meeting took place is our problem.

Taking into account all the asses we have in Ireland today of different colours, markings and other characteristics, it may be assumed that over the centuries all the different kinds intermingled through transcontinental trade routes. The traders themselves used asses for transport and these asses were hired at the different places that the caravans passed through en route. The Jewish tractate, *Baba Mesia*, testifies to this when it lays down the laws for the hiring of asses and ass drivers by contract, and regulates their foods and maximum loads. It is interesting to note that the animals from Lycaonia, now a part of modern Turkey, were the strongest of all breeds and thus best for long journeys.

These ancient trade routes wound their way across Asia from Nanking in eastern China to the Phoenician city of Tyre, and from there they continued either through Egypt and Libya over North Africa on the south or through Turkey and Greece on the north of the Mediterranean into Europe, and so over the years to Britain and Ireland, thus travelling through the habitats of most known Asiatic ass herds.

The routes that the African asses took are less well known. They certainly travelled westwards and then northwards across Africa to the Pillars of Hercules (Gibraltar). This can be deduced from the appearance of their descendants when we meet them in the countries traversed. We hear from Herodotus that

> there is a great belt of sand, stretching from Thebes in Egypt [about 500 miles from the Mediterranean] to the Pillars of Hercules. Along this belt, separated from one another by about ten days' journey, are little hills formed of lumps of salt, and from the top of each gushes a spring of cold, sweet water. Men live in the neighbourhood of these springs.

He also tells us that a Libyan tribe, who lived in a place that is now called Fezzan in Tripolitania, chased the holemen or troglodyte Ethiopians (Abyssinians) in horse-drawn chariots along that great desert belt. This indicates that from ancient times there must have been constant communication across the Nile between northeast Africa, the home of the African wild ass, and the Mediterranean, other than through Egyptian coastal routes. Before entering Europe via Spain and Italy, one must have encountered the North African wild ass whose existence we know of but whose description is based solely on the information from Mr Killgore.

Having eventually reached Spain by one way or another, these animals found a welcome and so with care developed into an excellent breed. Their offspring quite definitely found its way to Ireland, showing individual characteristics from indigenous sources, or combining them, but finally degenerating through neglect and inbreeding.

In England donkeys were known in the tenth century, for James Greenwood in *Wild Sports of the World* says that, during the time of Ethelred, the donkey is mentioned as a costly animal and even in the time of Elizabeth I it was considered to be as valuable as a well-bred horse.

2. The Batty Ass

THE PIEBALD or skewbald ass has not made its appearance in Ireland until fairly recent years, and until breeding records are kept for a period it is difficult to assess which colours blend together to produce certain results. From my limited experience I have found that white is the primary colour in piebald or skewbald breeding, and because of this I wonder if only in recent years have African and Asiatic asses ceased to meet as wayfarers and settled down long enough to produce, over the generations, broken-coloured progeny.

That there have been numerous stone and mousey-grey asses in these isles for many years is an accepted fact, and it is interesting to read in *Life at the Zoo* by C.J. Cornish (1894) that, in the Southern Forest (New Forest) there are many hundreds of semi-wild donkeys, as well as ponies, which are left to nature from year to year. The ponies are of every colour known in the annals of horse breeding, but the shaggy little donkeys are all of a uniform dark stone colour that never varies. He continues,

> Incidentally, looking at the beautiful wild asses from the Desert of Cutch [India], Southern Africa and Central Asia, which are exhibited at the zoo, one is tempted to wonder how it comes that the race in this country has been allowed to degenerate, instead of being retained as a strong and useful auxiliary to our unrivalled breed of horses.

With the information that these dark stone-grey donkeys remained the same colours when kept isolated over a period, I turned in other directions. It had always been of great interest to me why broken-coloured animals, including horses and cattle, around parts of the west of Ireland are referred to as 'batty', and after the arrival of our first broken-coloured donkeys, when the locals asked to see the 'batty asses', I decided to try to find the origin of the word. After fruitless enquiries around the country, I searched through books to see if there was any breed of these animals that might suggest such a name, and eventually the word 'Battak' appeared as the name of a Sumatra pony in a book printed in 1905. According to this book these ponies were bred in the Battak range of hills in Sumatra and were a regular export to Singapore, being on average 11.3 hands high and of many colours, with piebalds and skewbalds in the majority. The pure white were highly thought of and reserved exclusively for ownership by the local chieftains.

Could it be that some voyager had imported Battak ponies to these parts at some time and so provided us with the derivative word of 'batty' for all our broken-coloured stock? An exciting and not improbable thought! Continuing, I found that 'the original colour of the unimproved Battak ponies is said to have been mouse-grey, with a black stripe down the back', before the introduction of Arab blood. The main reason for cross-breeding was that all neighbouring and local princes, sultans, and chieftains coveted the pure white, red-eyed (albino) ponies, without any markings. These ponies could not be purchased by anyone other than the chiefs of the district, and the introduction of Arab blood, apart from changing their original colour, was to combine 'the fire and beauty of the Son of the Desert with the hardiness and endurance of the Battak pony'.

The Arab equine strain comprises many colours, including whites, greys, bays, chestnuts, browns, and blacks. These, when crossed with the original mousey-grey colour of the Battak ponies, seem to have produced the piebalds, skewbalds and roans, as well as introducing their own colourings. The occasional white, being so greatly prized, must have been crossed with a large variety of other colours in an effort to obtain and maintain a pure white strain, thereby throwing broken colours indiscriminately. Since these ponies in their original state seem to have been of a similar colour to the African ass, surely one has grounds for assuming that likewise the various ass colours have been produced in spite of the reverse of the African and Asiatic species—it will be remembered from the previous chapter that the African ass was, broadly speaking, of mouse-grey shades with a black dorsal stripe, and the Asiatic ass white, chestnut and bay brown. Supposing this assumption to be correct, one wonders why these broken colours have appeared only in recent years; it seems unbelievable that they have not met and bred before.

If the Battak ponies appeared as broken-coloured as a result of crossing white Arabs with the original mouse-grey, black dorsal-striped stock in an effort to produce the pure white breed so highly prized by their chieftains, could it not be possible that crossing white asses with mousey or stone-grey ones would also produce broken colours? If so, the reason why this has taken so long to come about is that it is the sort of thing that only happens when selection of animals for mating is deliberately made over a period of time, and if it is accepted that white is a primary colour, one could hazard a guess as to the delay, in Ireland anyway, of producing piebalds.

White has never been a very popular colour in Ireland with cattle because they were less able to stand up to the rigours of the Irish climate, more susceptible to vermin, and subject to a complaint called 'white heifer disease', which caused them either to abort or to fail to conceive. Since the ass was owned chiefly by country people, the prejudice against the white cow can be assumed to have extended to the white ass, so that the white asses, like white cattle, were most probably gelded if males and seldom bred from if females.

In the ancestry of any broken-coloured asses that I have knowledge of, there has always been a white parent or ancestor, and the more white forebears there are in the lineage, the more likelihood of getting broken colours, so perhaps in earlier days the first white donkey to breed with our mousey-coloured asses produced foals that took completely after one parent or another. Once these two colours were in the strain, subsequent generations produced broken-coloured progeny, and the intervention of any other colour just added to the mixture. It is interesting to note that just as yellowish patches sometimes appeared on one species of onager (wild Asiatic ass), so this same yellowish colour appears in many broken-coloured asses today.

The first broken-coloured donkey I saw in Ireland was in Adare, County Limerick. He was bought from a well-known circus by the 6th Earl of Dunraven in 1950 for £40, which was then considered a very high price for a donkey. He was a beautifully marked gelding called Mr Buttons.

Another point of interest is the absence of black in the colourings of wild asses, except in their stripings, because this colour is certainly prevalent in our 'mixed-up' ass of today. It could be due to instances of melanism, or an excess of colouring matter in the skin, rather than colour gradation, or it may have been that the North African (Libyan) wild ass was black before either the African or Asiatic species added their strain to turn it into the dark brown colour now found so often in Europe, especially in Spain. That it appeared earlier than its piebald or skewbald relations is beyond doubt. The chestnut colour seems to have been imported here about 1906 from Egypt, and from it (or them) have sprung the relatively few chestnuts to be found at present in Ireland.

The hooves seem to be the first part of the animal to show signs of colour changes, and on our stud I noticed that broken-coloured donkeys had either broken-coloured hooves, white hooves, or a mixture of each, and never four black ones. On white donkeys I have seen either all black, all white, or broken-colours. An ordinary coloured, mouse-grey foal born to us one season by a skewbald sire out of a mid-brown mare had all broken-coloured hooves. With regard to the chestnuts, one mare called Rowan, who was by a chestnut sire out of a mouse-grey mare, had very pale hooves, while a chestnut yearling colt named Ard Ri, by a chestnut sire out of a cinnamon-coloured mare called Cinnamon, had deep chestnut hooves. It is notable that this colt also had deep chestnut-coloured skin surrounding his eyes, while the mare's was pink in the same area. A broken-coloured filly foal had one eye surrounded by black skin, the other by pink skin! She was by a piebald sire out of a grey-brown mare. Some donkeys at the stud had very

pronounced leg markings, as on the African wild
asses, though these markings came on mouse-greys,
mid-brown, and dark brown-coloured animals. There
are many other interesting individual differences of
appearance, such as stiff manes, bifurcating shoulder
stripes and colour spots. Surely colour characteristics
appear and disappear according to cross-breeding:
Darwin's theory of 'colour being but a fleeting characteristic' cannot be applicable to our ass family. The
colour changes must be the result of the cross-breeding itself, according to the Mendelian theory of
heredity.

Donkeys have been crossed with zebras and the
offspring show many different markings. I have seen
a photograph of a young zebrass, the foal of a zebra
sire and donkey mare. It had a plain body, except for
the dorsal stripe and cross, with legs and ears striped
like a zebra. When the sire is a donkey and the dam a
zebra, the offspring is called a zebronkey, and sometimes collectively they are called zedonks. An interesting instance of cross-breeding mentioned by W.B.
Tegetmeier took place in the London Zoo towards
the end of the nineteenth century. A grey African wild
ass mare when mated for the first time was crossed
with a reddish-coloured Asiatic wild ass and produced a foal of similar colour to that of the male parent. (Incidentally, this offspring later entered the
Dublin Zoo.) Subsequently, the mare was mated three
times with an African wild ass of her own species and
produced three foals. The first two of these bore the

colour and markings common to their African species, but the last was of a reddish fawn colour, with white blaze and star markings on the face, the shorter ears of the Asiatic ass, and only the slightest indication of shoulder and leg stripes. Altogether a very unusual mixture.

Mr C.L. Sutherland, who was very well known in connection with the breeding of equines and their hybrids, stated that he had never seen these face markings, so common in the horse, on any of the many thousand asses that he had seen in Europe and North America. Whatever may have been the cause of these markings in that particular foal, their rarity just over a century ago was of great interest to me because they are not infrequently seen today, which appears to be evidence that the Asiatic and African strains are becoming more generally intermingled.

Quite apart from that, however, Tegetmeier draws attention to the curious fact that this latest foal resembled not its own parents but the stallion with whom its mother was first mated and says,

> Now, the question that presents itself is whether this is an accidental variation such as occurs from time to time in almost all animals, especially those in confinement of domestication, or whether it is an instance of the influence of a previous impregnation.

Without answering the question, he felt the facts of the case were worth putting on record.

It is seldom that donkeys have twins born alive

but, again, according to Sutherland, they conceive twins more frequently than do horses. In many cases, he states, these are the result of superfetation as is evidenced by the difference in size of the produce which, alas, the mare nearly always aborts. Successive matings are, or course, much more likely to occur among donkeys left to lead a natural life than among horses whose breeding has for so long been a matter of careful control.

In 1971 our first twins were born: Ome and Omi, a dark brown colt and a broken-coloured filly. Our Twinnies were a delight to all who knew them. Inseparable all twenty-six years of their life, so they were in death, for when one was faced with an incurable malady and had to go, it was unthinkable to separate them.

Other twins arrived later, two conspicuously marked broken-coloured colts, and though perfectly formed and delivered by a veterinarian, both were stillborn. This was owing to the mare being chased wantonly by children who, I learned afterwards, had broken into her field the night before she foaled. A third set of brown twins were born but sadly did not long survive.

Some less noticeable peculiarities of the ass family are the presence of callosities, sometimes known as chestnuts or castors, on the forelegs alone; and vestigial teats on the sheath of the male ass. I understand also that the ass has only five loin vertebrae as against six in the horse.

The life of the donkey is certainly long in domesticity; hence the expression 'donkey's years ago'. Animals of more than thirty years of age are not uncommon and even those in their forties and fifties are encountered; the kind of life they have led, as may be expected, contributes greatly to their longevity.

3. Introduction to Ireland

A FTER THE FOREGOING chapters in which the ancient lineage of the ass has been discussed, it will be a surprise to learn that the animal is a comparative newcomer to Ireland's shores. In spite of the fact that it has become a symbol of the country and is invariably depicted, along with leprechauns, harps and spinning wheels, as an integral part of peasant life, there are relatively few mentions of it before the eighteenth century.

An article on the Irish Levies in the Scottish wars from 1296 to 1302 in *The Irish Sword* states that £2 12s. 8d. was expended in Ayr on five asses to carry the money to pay the troops on campaign. There is a possibility that the returning Irish soldiers brought a few of these convenient beasts of burden home with them for use in their own, very similar country and that they were introduced in this way.

In 1642 we find in Mr Bagwell's *Ireland under the Stuarts* the captors of Maynooth Castle registering a complaint that they only got the benefit of one ass in their loot.

The only Irishman to have done any research in this field is Rev. J.P. Mahaffy, who read a paper to the Royal Irish Academy in 1917: 'On the Introduction of the Ass as a Beast of Burden into Ireland'. He states that he has been told positively by our specialists in Irish that there is no reference to them to be found in early Irish life, with the exception of artistic representations of the Flight into Egypt and the Ride of Jesus into Jerusalem.

This statement is also made by P.W. Joyce in *A Social History of Ancient Ireland* where he quotes, 'the ass hardly figures at all in ancient Irish literature, so that it cannot have been much used', and by R.L. Praeger in *Natural History of Ireland*, who says that the ass was one of the latest animals to be used for domestic purposes, as well as by E. Estyn Evans in *Irish Heritage*: 'The ass, which one might suppose to be long-established, was in fact hardly known before the nineteenth century.' Rev. Mahaffy goes on to say that the first positive introduction of the animal into the country was about the middle of the eighteenth century, when the Royal Dublin Society offered prizes for the importing of the Spanish ass—but only as a sire to breed mules. Later on, from 1891 to 1923, the Congested District Board had schemes for the improvement of the breed of asses.

Asses are scarcely mentioned in any eighteenth-century books, with the exception of *The Life and*

Times of Lord Cloncurry, where one of the 'most prominent facts in the early history of Robert Lawless' is described thus: 'One fine frosty morning, in the year of our Lord 1720, a little boy from the mountains, accompanied by a small ass-load of turf and firs, might be seen wending his way through the Liberty of Dublin, where three or four of his principal patrons resided.' Nor are they referred to in the records of the walled cities, which exacted tolls for all the animals and all the produce that entered their gates, although in 1723 and subsequently a Mr Westropp had found advertisements in Dublin papers of milch-asses.

In the Irish Acts of Parliament, there is a mention of the animal in 1743. Act 17 holds out a threat of death for anyone tempted to 'Kill, cut open, or skin any cow, calf, etc., sheep or lamb, or any horse, mare, gelding, colt, filly, ass, or mule, with intent to steal the fat, flesh, skin, or carcase thereof', particularly if they were so untidy as to leave the carcass on the high road in the vicinity of Dublin. Professor Mahaffy does not lay much stress on this evidence though, since he thinks it may well have been copied from an English act. He prefers to accept as definite the institution of a 20s. tax imposed on 'any person travelling with any horse or horses, ass or asses, mule or mules, or any other beast or beasts drawing burthen', in Acts 23 and 24, in 1783.

Also, there is John Rutty's observation in 'An Essay Towards the Natural History of the County of

Dublin', published in 1772, that 'the female ass is of no small use for its milk in populous and distempered cities, though better supplied from places at a distance, where their food is less succulent'. Primate Boyle, a well-known member of the Cork and Orrory family, would seem to bear out this assertion, for he often had an ass accompany him for the sake of its milk. He died in 1702, having lived to well over ninety years of age.

With such sources of information available, it is surprising that Arthur Young, a most observant writer who made a detailed study of Ireland in the mid-1770s, should have remained completely silent on the ass. Rev. Mahaffy expressly refers to his astonishment at this lack of information from such a careful author.

It also seems strange that in the statistical surveys, which were organized about 1800 by the Royal Dublin Society and carried out in five counties by Sir Charles Coote, asses were only found by him in Monaghan. A sentence from his report reads:

Asses are also very numerous here. Frequently 100 of these animals may be counted in the busy seasons, within the circuit of a mile or two. They are found extremely serviceable and are very easily fed. They are particularly fond of the tops of furze and green whins.

Few of the other surveys have mention of them, apart from passing references to mules, excepting the

ones for Clare and Galway by Hely Dutton. The
Clare survey was published in 1808 and these sen-
tences are at the end:

> Very great use is made of mules and asses for carry-
> ing baskets and small loads, such as poor people
> usually load them with; for such persons as are not
> able to keep a horse they are a great convenience. It
> is astonishing what a load these little asses will carry,
> frequently twenty-four stone, much more than their
> own weight.

The Cork survey was published seven years later
and the author of this comments on the small size of
the mules, remarking that they are 'got by the common jackass'.

Taking all in all, Rev. Mahaffy comes to the con-
clusion that the animal was of little or no account
until the first decade of the nineteenth century. He
thinks it unlikely that the first trade in asses was
through travellers, as some people have suggested,
but mentions an old man who was said to have made
his livelihood by going to Scotland and thence
importing asses to the north of Ireland, and on to the
west. This may have been during the time of the Penin-
sular War (1808–13) to which the British expedition
started from Cork. He points out that this war obviously caused a great drain on Irish horses, which were
required for cavalry, draught, and transport, and the
resulting depletion gave an advantage to those who
offered the ass as a cheap and safe substitute.

Whatever the reason, the Registrar-General's Returns of the numbers of livestock in Ireland for 1841 shows that there were 92,356 asses, which by 1871 had increased to 180,024.

Originally I had found no earlier references to the ass in Ireland than the one in the complaint by the captors of Maynooth Castle in 1642, referred to by Rev. Mahaffy. The first step was only an allusion emanating from a book published in Dublin by John K'eogh in 1739 called *Zoologia Medicinalis Hibernica, or a Treatise of Birds, Beasts, Fishes, Reptiles or Insects, which are commonly known and propagated in this Kingdom. Giving an account of their Medicinal virtues and names in English, Irish and Latin.* In this treatise the Irish name for the ass is *assile*, and one finds three pages of medicinal advice on the use of nearly every component part of this animal. Surely this suggests such a demand as to leave the reader wondering if there were a multitude of asses around the country at that time, less than a century apart from the single captive at Maynooth Castle in 1642.

Of special interest in the current investigation is the apparent lack of an early Irish (Gaelic) word for the ass. An indication of this is noted by Professor Myles Dillon of the Dublin Institute of Advanced Studies in his commentary on the tenth-century poem 'Saltair na Rann', i.e. 'The Book of Adam and Eve in Ireland', where the writer, in telling the story of Balaam's ass, uses the word *lair*, which translates as 'mare'.

Professor Fergus Kelly, a senior professor of Celtic

Studies at the Institute, quotes in his recently published monumental book *Early Irish Farming*, the
occasional usage in early Irish of the word '*as(s)an*, a
borrowing from the Latin *asinus*'. He observes that in
later Irish this was replaced by *as(s)al* from the Latin
diminutive *assellus*. He also refers to the word *assain*
used in a twelfth-century narrative.

In the fifteenth century the usage of *asal* can be
found in the *Book of Ballymote* and in a 1475 Irish
version of the travels of Sir John Manderville, '*baine
essai*' denotes asses' milk.

Incidentally, what is very possibly the earliest use
of *asal* in a place-name comes from John O'Donovan
in his mid-nineteenth-century translation of the
thousand-year-old *Book of Rights*. Here he cites
Cnoc Droma Assail as the original name of Tory Hill,
which stands just outside of Croom in County Limerick.

Rejoining the ass again on the road backwards in
time, we have reached a resting place, and as far as
we can see, most probably journey's end as well, with
information gleaned once more from Professor Kelly.
Here he states that, to the best of his knowledge, 'the
earliest explicit reference to an ass on Irish soil is in
an anecdote in a legal manuscript', and he goes on to
quote from one of three manuscript versions to be
found in the library of Trinity College Dublin.

These record how a cardinal came from Rome to
give instructions to certain ecclesiastics, but several
members of his audience, not liking what he had to

say, stole his '*eich agus muil agus asain*', in other words, the cardinal's horses, mules and asses. This incident is alleged to have taken place in the reign of Domnall Mór Ua Briain, king of Munster, who died in 1194.

The background to this theft is based upon a real historic event. In 1177, eight years after the Norman Invasion, a Papal Legate, Cardinal Vivian, came to this country and summoned an ecclesiastical synod to convene at Dublin. There he laid down the duty of the Irish people, on pain of excommunication, to pay allegiance to Henry II, the English king, as the true and rightful lord of Ireland. Thus, the subsequent reaction of some members of his audience is understandable.

As for the asses, surely we can conclude our research to date, by accepting them as, at least, mediaeval immigrants?

However, it is a pleasant conceit that the first major description of the ass in printed English literature is to be found in a book that was composed in Ireland. In 1574, Barnaby Googe, a distinguished English classical scholar, was sent to Ireland by his cousin, Sir William Cecil, afterwards the first Lord Burghley, to look after the family estates. He remained in the country for eleven years, eventually becoming Lord President of Connacht.

While in Ireland, he undertook a major translation, namely *Foure Bookes of Husbandrie*, of a recently published collection of farming advice that had been gathered together by Conrad Heresbach, Counsellor to the Duke of Cleves. As the title page signifies, this had been 'newly Englished and increased' when it was first published in 1577. Thereafter it was frequently reprinted, achieving recognition as one of the great Elizabethan agricultural books.

In 'The third booke entreating of Cattell', the horse-keeper is told that he has spoken enough on the subject of horses and that 'it is time you say something of asses'. To this the horse-keeper makes a lengthy response:

> It is greatly out of order, but since you will needes have me so to doe, I will not sticke with you to say what I can therein, that eche of you may doe the like in his charge.
>
> Asses are commonly kept, yet not to bee little set by, because of their sundry commodities, and the hardnesse of their feeding, for this poore beast contents himselfe with what meate so ever you give him, Thistles, Bryers, Stalkes, Chaffe, wherefore every countrey hath store, is good meate with him; besides, he may best abide the ill looking to of a negligent keeper, and able to sustaine blowes, labor, hunger and thirste, being seldom or never sicke, and therefore of all cattell longest endureth: for being a beast nothing chargeable, he serveth for a number of necessary uses: in carrying of burdens he is comparable to the Horse, he draweth the Cart (so the lode be not unreasonable): for grinding in the Mill he passeth all others, therefore in the countrey the Asse is most useful for carrying of things to the market, and Corne to the Mill.

In Egypt and Barbary (where the ground is very light) they have also their use in plowing: and the fine Ladies of the country doo ride upon Asses richely furnished: yea, they be very apt to be taught, so as at this day in Alcayre you shall have them dance very manerly, and keepe measure with their Musitian. Varro maketh mention of two sortes, one wilde, whereof in Phrigia and Lycaonia there are great store: the wild Asses that are tamed are passing good, specially for breed & they are easely broken: the other is tame, of which I meane to speake.

The best are brought of Arcadia (although Varro seems to commend the breede of Italy for goodnesse). He that will have a breede of Asses, must have the male and female both of reasonable age, large bodied, sound and of a good kind: the male must be at least three yeeres old, for from three, till they be tenne, they be fit for breeding: they bring foorth their Coltes sometimes at two yeeres and a halfe, but three yeeres is the best age: the female goeth as long with her burden as the Mare, and dischargeth in all respectes as she doeth: but she will not very well retain, except she be forced immediately after the horsing to runne about.

She seldome bringeth foorth two. When she foaleth, she gets her into some darke place, and keepes her selfe from being seene. They will beare all their life time, which as Aristotle saith is thirtie yeeres: they are put to the horse a little before the tenth of June and beare every other yeere: they bring foorth their fole at the twelvemonth. While they be with Fole they must not bee greatly laboured, for hazarding their Fole: the male must never be idle, for he is as lecherous as the devill, and by rest will waxe naught.

The colt is suffered to run with the damme the first yeere, & the next is gently tied up with her, only in the night time: the third yeere they are broken, according to their use. The damme doth wonderfully love her young so much, as she will not sticke to come through the fire to it: but the water she dare in no wise come neare, no not to touch it with her foote, neither will she drinke in any strange water, but where she is used to watered, and so as she may goe & stand dry foote.

They delight to be lodged in wide roomes, & are troubled with fearefull dreames in their sleepes, whereat they so pawe with their legges, that if they lie neere any hard thing, they hurte their feete: in drinking, they scarsely touch the water with their lippes (as it is thought) for feare of wetting their goodly eares, whose shadowes they see in their drinking: no beast can worse away with colde then this. If your Asses halt at any time, you shall thus remedy them. Wash all the foote with warme water, & afterwards make them clean with a sharp knife which when you have donne, take old chamber lye, as hot as may be & melt therein goates suet; or if you have not that, Oxe tallow, & anoint all the feete til they be hole.

What renders this such a remarkable historical document is that it shares a common first edition date with the celebrated set of chronicles compiled by Raphael Holinshed. In Holinshed's extensive topography of England, the ass and his relations are curtly dismissed in the following brief sentence: 'Our land doeth yeeld no asses and therefore we want the generation of mules.'

In spite of his reluctance to 'say something of asses', the horse-keeper quoted by Barnaby Googe had plenty to say and elucidated their temperament and management with accuracy and perceptive consideration. Some characteristic traits and habits mentioned reminded me of lessons we had to learn the hard way. Sadly, we found young foals could 'worse away with cold' unless sheltered during inclement weather. In the early days the selective drinking habits of our donkeys at the stud, particularly lactating mares, propelled us into constant action, refilling buckets with fresh water, until we produced self-filling bowls.

As for the stallions, they certainly were 'lecherous as the devill' and would face the walls of China to reach interesting mares.

The ass appears to have been introduced into Britain before the Norman Conquest and there is evidence that its use continued in Scotland at least up to the fourteenth century. Whether it was continuous thereafter, I know not. But in England it seems almost to have died out, for in the days of Elizabeth I asses were very scarce and valuable. In the reign of Henry VIII great efforts were made to improve the breeding of horses for transport, and indeed a statute of 1535 required the killing and burying of all mares as were not likely to produce stock fit for profitable labour.

It seems to me not improbable that at a time when only the best horses were allowed to survive, the ass's chance of survival grew dim, unless in the capacity of a milch-ass. And considering their scarcity in England, it would be hard to believe that they were numerous in Ireland even as late as 1642.

Personally, I suspect that over here they were originally used for milking purposes by the wealthy before becoming the poorer man's horse.

4. Uses in Ireland

NO ANIMAL EVER fitted into the country of its adoption or the way of life of its people so well as the donkey, which has now become, like many a human settler over the ages, more Irish than the Irish. The small, strong, sturdy little immigrant soon proved to be the ideal helpmate to the native farmer, struggling for existence among the rocks and bogs in the wild counties of Ireland. Innumerable uses were found for this creature, which could survive and work on terrain that was out of the question for a horse—which the people in most cases could not afford, anyway.

In the beginning, as we have already seen, ass's milk was discovered to be good for TB and gout, and also the complexion, if it came from a recently foaled mare that had not been mated again, and was drunk before it had been allowed to grow cold. In fact, we once had a letter from a woman in County Monaghan asking for a small bottle of ass's milk to cure an ulcer on her leg! But sometimes the ass had a more frivolous role to play and as early as 1776 it was giving a good performance in a travelling circus—a role that is still fulfilled by a similar animal today.

According to Constantia Maxwell, another of its early jobs in Ireland was one that certainly contributed to history, for Bianconi began his famous long car passenger service with an ass-drawn vehicle. Having thus proved its usefulness in no mean fashion, future jobs were not slow in coming its way. Its dung had already been found to be excellent manure for strong or moist land and the donkey was soon to supplement its own supply by the drawing of seaweed, which is still highly valued as a fertilizer for potatoes on the sandy soil of low-lying coasts.

This wrack was mostly thrown up during storms, but sometimes had to be added to by cutting and pulling the weed from the rocks, each family having a carefully laid out portion of the shore to harvest. It was carried up to the beach by means of back-creels and hand-barrows, where it was stacked ready for the carts and creel-asses to draw away.

Several variations in the method of transport of this seaweed and other goods were used. The basket panniers were probably the most common form, as neither road nor level ground was necessary for their employ. They were made by taking two scraws of grass about 3" thick and 2" square, which were put one over the other. Then eight rods were selected from a bundle of approximately 250 hazel rods 6" long and were placed firmly, two together, in each corner. Two more were placed next in a similar way every 3", when the weaving was commenced also with two rods together to start with, then singly for 3" and double again for about 1". At that stage a 3" space was left to enable the basket to be lifted when full, after which the rods were carried across the space and woven double for another 5", when the rods were bent over at right angles and woven until all the ends were used up to make the bottom of the basket. When completed, the basket was lifted off the scraw of grass and a pair of straw mats was woven to put across the ass's back, with a straddle consisting of two pieces of wood held together by three strips of iron and having two iron pegs in the centre to hold the baskets. The basket was often constructed with a hinged bottom as well, which allowed the contents to be easily unloaded.

On occasions when, for some reason or another, creels were dispensed with and the load was placed directly on the ass, a simple *súgán* was made consisting of a ring of straw some fifteen inches in diameter and bound with a fine straw rope. This was a variant of the head-wreath once widely worn in Western Europe as a carrying pad.

Also instead of creels in the 'slipe', a type of sled was sometimes used that could easily be dragged over rough, boulder-strewn hillsides and was useful for transporting the plough or the harrow from field to field across land that was too steep or too sodden for wheeled vehicles. This method is still employed for such tasks where no better means of transport has yet been devised.

Between the 'slipe' and the cart came the slide car, a simple conveyance made from two parallel poles that served both as shafts and runners and were fastened together by crosspieces to form a carrying platform. Once widely used, this is now confined to Ulster mainly for the transport of turf from mountain bogs down steep tracks to valley farms.

In the great days of kelp-burning, the ass played no small part and all along the west coast where Laminaria seaweed was cut, the money to be made depended entirely upon the beast of burden. The cutting was done in deep water by the men, whose knives and sickles would sometimes be fitted with handles twenty feet long, after which the women and children, their backs protected from the damp by goatskins, would carry the weed in back-creels to where the ass was waiting to take over.

Kelp-burning takes place no longer, but the salty harvest has other uses today: ribbon weed and rods yield the algin that is used in textile manufacture for the making of nylons, and as a thickener for soups, jellies, ice cream and paints, as well as for the substance used for taking dental impressions; bladder wrack suffers a sea change into animal foods and soap; and carrageen is used for making sweets.

More and more the economy of the small farmer became bound up with his donkey: they were used in pairs, as in Donegal, for ploughing, and slinging hay was another small but vital task. It consisted of a rope being passed around the small cocks of hay in a field, then fastened to the animal, which pulled them to where the large cock was being made at one end. We at home did this with a horse, but elsewhere donkeys were used. The milk, too, from the small farms was brought by means of the donkey and cart to the creamery, the great social meeting place of the farmers, where each day the news of the district was given and received. The shopping was done in this way, either in a box cart with low sides about one foot high and a plank across known as a pleasure seat, or in a trap; pigs and sheep were brought in the cart to the fairs, which still take place in the main streets of the western towns, or turf was transported in the cart now fitted with higher sides, or creels; while for carrying loads such as hay or sticks sides like curved gates, known as 'yards', were fitted.

For those who could afford a good cart and harness there was an opportunity to exhibit at the Spring Show, as for many years the Royal Dublin Society had a class for donkeys shown in harness. Unfortunately, though, this was not a great success, since most of the donkey-owners in the country were unable to afford the niceties of tackling!

Sometimes the willingness of the poor beast was very much overtaxed, though John Mills writes in 1776 that, 'In proportion to his size, he will carry a heavier load than perhaps any other animal, nor is

there a more easy going or sure footed animal.' By
1830 Martin Doyle was writing,

> I should much prefer an ass to a horse for a small
> holder; the loads which he will draw on a level road
> with a well constructed cart are surprisingly great;
> on some of the colliery roads, though hilly, as from
> Castlecomer to Kilkenny, half a ton weight of coals
> is often drawn by an ass; this is, however, excessively
> cruel: the horse is forced to draw a ton or twenty-
> five cwt. on the same roads: the consequence is that
> both animals are soon destroyed.

This description might well apply to an overloaded
donkey of today being used on the farm or by travellers, who were not slow to add the animal to the ret-
inue of their corps. A colourful, if not exactly com-
forting, picture of the latter is painted for us by Maurice Walsh in *The Road to Nowhere*:

> The clack and squeak of many ungreased axles came
> from the road, and over the crown of the high-
> cocked bridge poured a ragged regiment of tinkers.
> There were half a dozen ass-drawn carts, piled with
> women, children, crooked poles, old sacking, osier-
> work baskets, gleaming tins; a dust-covered scamp
> sat in the front of each cart, feet dangling at each
> side of the donkey's croup, and, at regular intervals,
> as a mere matter of routine a dangling foot kicked
> the animal in the belly—and the animal took no
> notice. Bringing up the rear was a whole drove of
> donkeys, all colours, all shapes, all ages, but not a
> decently-bred one among the lot.

Over the ages the donkey has catered for a variety of human requirements and though we often hear of his daily tasks we seldom hear of the useful purposes he fulfils after his death. One of our strangest possessions, for instance, is a backgammon set made from the skin of an ass! This skin, being very hard and elastic, has been used for making drums, sieves, pocketbooks and even strong shoes. Shagreen, an untanned or lightly tanned leather obtained from the rump and buttocks of the animal (the best coming from the wild ass), used to be much in demand for covering small articles such as requisites for the dressing table and the writing desk, cigarette boxes, sword hafts, photograph frames, etc. The surface of shagreen was rough with tiny round lumps, the best being grey. It was usually dyed green, however, and less frequently blue, red or black.

Despite the Greek proverb in which the man who expects to reap where he has not sown is laughed at, as one who looks for wool on an ass, I have got our donkey hair spun into wool, with the help of a kind and interested friend in Devon. If somewhat coarse, it appears suitable for the weaving of mats, rugs, bags and perhaps even toy donkeys! Anyway, experimenting with it was fun, but overall not a great success.

5. Birth of a Stud Farm

WHEN WE BOUGHT our place in Clare early in the 1960s we certainly never thought that very soon it would be the headquarters of a 'Donkey Stud'. Such are the surprises of life, and it is a certainty that donkey stud life is full of surprises. With less than two acres of land around the house, and of that only a small paddock in front of the house suitable for grazing, we thought it would be fun to buy a couple of donkey mares; they would initially keep each other company and, after suitable marriages, give us the pleasure of foals which, when weaned, we could sell and then we could breed some more.

As a family we have always been fond of animals and in our childhood home at Midleton, County Cork, we were surrounded by them, both in the house and outside. There were donkeys in all the neighbouring homesteads. Later on, after my marriage, living between north-west Cork and Kerry, we kept horses and through hunting, point-to-pointing and racing, travelled fairly extensively around the countryside where the donkey was much in evidence.

After some years in England, mostly during the 1950s, I returned to Ireland to find, naturally enough, many changes, although our soft-coloured countryside was as quietly beautiful as ever—apart from the many empty spaces in field and bog, by cottages and even on the roadside, which had once been filled by donkeys, whose silhouettes and vague colours were always an integral part of the Irish scenery.

When the time came for the big decision as to what animal should honour our small paddock it was not difficult, when aided by the thought of the small financial outlay entailed, to decide on *Equus asinus*. Our next move and only other expense, so we thought, was to put up a fence to shut off the paddock from the driveway, and with this quickly accomplished two grey-brown mares duly arrived: although there was then no thought further from our minds, the Spanish Point Donkey Stud in County Clare had started.

Of course, once you have a donkey you must give him shelter, especially when you live right on the Atlantic coast with no trees or hedges. Even more essential is a nice tank of clean water in the paddock. Also necessary is some hay for the winter months, a fork with which to lift it and a spade and brush to clean out the shelter. One could not possibly do without a headcollar and some grooming equipment.

Imagine not having a stable in case they got ill? And I'm quite sure no one ever kept a donkey without a cart. As for a cart without harness, well, that is unheard of. Not forgetting to mention that a bridle and saddle are also useful if there are small children about. Perhaps it was understandable that my husband remarked that to own a donkey one must be as rich as Croesus—a remark that resulted in the naming of one of our first donkeys Miss Croesus.

All went according to our original plan for a short while and then two things happened together, followed a little later by a third to catapult us into business. Somebody mentioned that though grey asses were very nice, they preferred brown and black ones. This remark, coinciding with the news that some nearby fields could be purchased, was enough to propel us into further action and soon both fields and dark asses were acquired.

Once again we rested, happy with our lot, until a friend sent us a photograph of a skewbald or piebald donkey about to leave Dublin docks for England. We were fascinated by it and felt that one like it must be added to our number. Well, after many enquiries and advertisements in various newspapers for 'an unusual-coloured donkey', we bought a pretty little skewbald filly of about nine months old. It was the fact of her price being so astonishingly in excess of the price paid for one-colour donkeys, combined with the intense interest we had as to how they were bred, that really decided us to start a stud farm.

After that everything snowballed: more land, more donkey mares and fillies and, perhaps the most important ingredient of a stud farm, some handsome and well bred stallions, until we reached our final strength of more than a hundred animals (not including the visiting mares to the stallions) and about forty acres of land, plus more held under lease.

In 1968, we had four stallions of different colours at service: a white, a piebald, a skewbald and a dark grey/black. In addition, we had a handsome chestnut colt. All were bred in Ireland, with the exception of the skewbald, Pepito. For some time we believed him to have been bred in Ireland, but later found out he had, in fact, been bred in England.

At first we felt it a great handicap not to have all our land together around the house. Instead we had odd fields here and there, with the largest acreage quite a distance from the house, but we soon discovered it to be an asset. Our long-eared friends with their strident bray could call to each other from a great distance and this complicated stud life in many ways, especially at mating and weaning times. This is mainly because stallions do not get on with each other and cannot be kept together in the same field as they will fight fiercely, particularly if there is a mare 'in season' (ready for mating) anywhere near. Unless the fields were exceptionally well fenced I could not even keep them in adjoining fields in the mating season.

Once, off-season, when we were very short of grass, I put two stallions in separate fields that only touched at one well-fenced corner. Both animals immediately galloped to their respective adjoining corners and with a wild lashing of tails snorted violent abuse at each other. Having said all they could think of without any physical harm being done, they went and refreshed themselves on what grass there was to offer, returning many times each and every day to continue the altercation in case there was anything left unsaid. We were often asked whether it was safe to allow a stallion to be in the same field as mares with foals at foot. Our reply was 'get to know your stallion well first'. Many stallions are safe enough to be allowed to join in family life, but not all. A stallion will stay very happily with any number of mares, and also with a gelding, if they have been brought up together, though whether this includes the mating season, I do not know, because in the only instance of this that we experienced the gelding and stallion lived happily together until just before they were two years old when, to our great distress, the gelding died suddenly.

With regard to foals and stallions together, my first two experiments were not encouraging. They were both with different stallions and foals, and in both cases the stallions rushed towards the foals, in one instance frightening the foal so much that it jumped through a nearby wire fence—luckily, to our astonishment, without injury. On the second occasion we were quick enough to catch the stallion before he had rushed too far, not daring to risk his intentions.

However, we had a happier experience when our

stallion Dubh'sbán broke into a paddock full of mares with both colt and filly foals at foot. It was with great trepidation that I viewed this situation until I witnessed the following incident from my window. The stallion, while making preliminary mating overtures to the mare in season, was interrupted by a foal who wanted to drink. Fully expecting trouble for the little one, I was about to rush out to intervene when to my amazement the stallion, ceasing his attentions to the mare, quietly grasped the foal by its neck, first pulling and then pushing it firmly though gently out of the way before returning to continue his amorous activities. His gentlemanly conduct lasted for the rest of his sojourn amongst them. All our stallions were extremely friendly to us and to our visitors, coming up to be petted and talked to as soon as we came in sight.

At weaning time also we found it convenient that distance separated our fields because it is much kinder to both mares and foals if they are kept far away from each other, as with their long ears they can hear for a long distance, and if they hear no reply to their pathetic calls, they will more quickly get used to their enforced separation. So, in spite of the obvious disadvantages of so much 'to-ing and fro-ing' on a scattered farm, it has decided advantages when dealing with donkeys *en masse*.

From our house, which was on the crest of a hill, we were able to keep an eye on the stock in nearly all our local fields with the aid of binoculars. This

enabled us to see if a mare answered when the stallion called, one of the indications that she was in season, and also if a mare had started to foal, or if they
had broken out of their fields, or any other unusual
happenings needing attention, all this helping to minimize our labour. These advantages, added to the
knowledge that in each field there was a comfortable
shelter where the donkeys could hide from the rigours
of our temperamental weather along this magnificent
Atlantic coast, made us feel that the pros far out-
numbered the cons for a donkey stud, where we never
expected to have one, in the wild west of Ireland.

6. A Stud Year

STARTING OUR LOOK AT stud life at the beginning of the calendar year, January would find all animals in their fields, a stallion among a herd of 'in foal' mares in various fields, and younger stock together in other fields unless, of course, we had the misfortune to have an invalid (this can happen in the best of families), which had to be stabled for the winter. Each field had a shelter with good ventilation; a salt lick, which is a help in controlling worms—a subject that will be dealt with later; a hay rack for supplementary feeding; some troughs of the kind used for feeding pigs in which we gave the donkeys pony nuts in small quantities as an extra supplementary; and hay ricks as near to the shelters as possible. We kept both the troughs and the hay convenient to a gateway in order to minimize labour.

Clean, fresh water is a commodity much appreciated by donkeys as they are the daintiest of drinkers, not plunging their noses into the water as horses do (some sages maintain from the fear of seeing the shadow of their ears), but stretching their necks and touching the water gently with their lips, thus allowing themselves to breathe freely as they drink. Our water tanks were fitted with ballcocks or small bowls with a lever that caused them to fill up when pushed gently by the animals' noses, both these being labour-saving and ensuring fresh water.

Around February or early March we started feeding rolled oats to the stallions in preparation for the mating season, which usually begins in March or April. As we took visiting mares to our stallions, they had to be kept fitter than those who only had their home work to attend to.

Then came the most exciting time of the year, the foaling season, mostly between April and July on our stud. As their time drew nearer we separated these mares from the others and kept them in fields close by our house.

About six weeks before foaling the mare's udder begins to get larger, but this varies greatly as we did have maiden mares who made only the slightest 'springing', as this is called, before foaling. Nearer her time, as the foal positions itself for birth, the ligaments near the base of the tail relax, disclosing little valleys in the rump, and her vulva or bearing begins to lengthen and swell. Some mares show a slight waxy substance at the end of each teat and when this happens the animal should foal during the next twenty-four hours, but this is not always a reliable sign because other mares do not show this at all, and others can trick you by showing it much too early.

So many donkey owners tell me that they have never seen their donkeys foaling that one presumes they foal at night-time. This brings the owners a delightful awakening, except on the occasion when something goes wrong when, being unforewarned of the event, it has been impossible to avoid tragedy. Luckily this does not often happen, but with first foalers, or mares with a previous difficulty, we observed them at intervals both day and night. The danger can be that though the mare has safely delivered her foal, she can be quite bewildered by the experience and remain sitting for so long that by the time she has regained her equilibrium sufficiently to pay attention to the foal, it may have gotten smothered because it did not manage to break through the membrane bag that encloses the body at birth. Having lost a piebald foal in these circumstances, and having heard of other similar losses, I found it advisable to take this rather time-consuming care even though often after many nocturnal visits the little creature arrived safely in broad daylight.

Many more of our mares foaled during the day than at night and while watching them in their discomfort was obviously a help to practical experience, I found it no help at all to my emotional life!

Allowing for a normal birth, we noticed as a preliminary sign that a mare sits down to rest more often than usual; then, when the time for birth is imminent, she wanders around the paddock in an unsettled manner until she suddenly flops down and labour commences. The mare may get up and flop down many times, perhaps even grazing at intervals during labour. A bag will appear (looking at first like a large bubble) then within it the forelegs of the foal start to show, one foot a little in advance of the other, followed by the head, nose first, and the neck. She then rests before further effort produces the trunk. She may do this standing, though more often lying down. Meanwhile, the foal will have commenced to wriggle awkwardly; it is a help to pull apart the membrane over its nose to enable it to breathe. Finally, after resting again, the mare will deliver the foal. The time from commencement of birth to delivery should be about half to three-quarters of an hour—possibly a little longer for maidens and old mares—but if after that time birth has not started, or the foal is appearing in a way other than that just described, call your vet immediately, for his speedy attention is now essential, and delay could cost the life of mare and foal.

After birth the foal will rest for a while and the cord attached to it should break at the narrow end near its body. If this does not happen after an appreciable time it can be cut away with sterilized scissors—first tie the cord about two inches from the body with some sterilized gut. The mare should then cleanse herself of the afterbirth, but if this does not take place by three or four hours after the birth, the vet must be called in to remove it.

The newcomer will now be trying to stand up with the most astonishing and terrifying series of acrobatics; those little legs shoot in all directions and send the body lurching here and there, sometimes landing it in such a knot of legs, head, and body, that it looks impossible to unwind. After numerous attempts, often with the bright idea of using its nose as a fifth leg, or perhaps a helpful nudge from Mum in the right place, it makes its first wobbly stand, followed shortly by its first wobbly steps.

All this exercise will have helped to remove the small rubber-like substance that at birth is attached to each hoof to protect the mare from the hardness of the hooves in the womb and during birth.

Intermittently the mare will lick the foal and it will start looking for some food, seldom in the right place to start with, but eventually getting there. A nice bran mash consisting of a few handfuls of bran and a handful of rolled oats with a pinch of salt mixed with boiling water and allowed to cool is generally appreciated by the mare, who will then like to remain quietly with her new baby for some time. If there are other mares or foals in the field, they will be curious, but the mother is normally well able to protect her young. During bad weather we would bring the mare and foal into a stable. We seldom brought a mare in before foaling as they seemed happier to foal outside and, if the weather was bad, would foal in the shelter.

If, during the first few weeks of life, the weather was very wet, we used to watch to see that the foals did not get soaked, and often many dryings with a towel were necessary before the foal learned to stay under cover while the mare feeds. Many people may think this unnecessary, but in excessively bad weather the foal's coat is not yet waterproof enough to keep out the heavy rain and drenching that could precipitate a chill. This, I am sure, causes the loss of many Irish foals.

Most people say that in seven to ten days and up to three weeks after foaling, the mare will come in season again and be ready for mating, but many of our mares did not agree with that notion at all and had no intention of bothering about this time factor. They came in season just when they felt like it. Whether this was due to their physical fitness, the weather, or plain temperament I do not know, except that I noticed that they delayed more when the weather was cold. Otherwise they vary greatly in this matter, as well as to the actual time they remain in season, which is generally from four to six days, and even up to ten days. Also after mating it is thought that, if they have not conceived, they will 'come in' again after three weeks, but once again I found that many react individually, as well as according to plan.

A mare will come in season first when she is a two-year-old (and often earlier) and, all being well, will breed from then until she reaches a ripe old age. A possible exception to this is the three-year-old, at which age I have found many mares who come in season regularly are, whether having foaled previously or not, exceedingly difficult to breed from. I cannot think of any reason as to why this should be, unless they are preoccupied with changing teeth, a process with which they are deeply involved at that age.

When a mare has a foal with her, and if stallions are kept in the vicinity, it is easier to tell when a mare is in season than otherwise. If a foal starts scouring (diarrhoea) it could be the first indication, but care must be taken that the foal is not doing this for any other reason. The mare will become restive, sometimes sniff the air, and maybe bray to attract the attention of the stallion, who is very quick to answer. When he does it will cause the mare to react by making rhythmic motions with her mouth, and perhaps to stale, indicating that she is ready for mating. She may also behave like this with her mouth if there is no stallion nearby, and may not even call out, so unless one watches carefully it is often easy to miss their mating time. Many mares only show their in-season symptoms after hearing a bray from the stallion, who smells their effluvia. As our stallions brayed loudly and lustily it was quite a summer pastime, added to an already full curriculum, to run from window to window to see if a mare would answer!

We did not mate a mare immediately after we noticed she had come in unless we suspected that she may have been ready for mating before we discovered her condition. We generally waited a day or two before introducing her to the stallion. In fact, country people will tell you, 'She's at her best for breedin' when she's going off.' When the time was right our normal practice was to put the mare into a stable and then fetch whichever stallion was required for the service.

Immediately after service by the stallion it is advisable to walk the mare for some time, to prevent her from staleing, for this is an occasion when the action of staleing frequently causes her to eject the seminal fluid as well. A book published in Dublin in 1776 devotes a chapter to the most approved method in the breeding, rearing, and fitting for use of the ass. The following paragraph is most interesting:

> The ass is capable of generating so early as at the age of two years: the female is even sooner ripe than the male, and full as lascivious; for which reason she is a bad breeder, ejecting again the seminal fluid she has just received in coition, unless the sensation of pleasure be immediately removed by loading her with blows; the only method of preventing the consequences of her amorous convulsions. This is a precaution without which they would very seldom retain.

The courtship of these animals is frequently noisy, generally frenzied and by no means a gentle affair. It is surprising the hard kicks the stallion can take, and the hard bites he can give, without serious injury to either party.

As the gestation period for a donkey is about a year, sometimes under the year and often over it from a few days to a few weeks and even a month, we seldom mated our mares after July, to avoid late season foals. However, we continued with visiting mares, which came from more sheltered places, until well on into the autumn.

Our fillies varied as to the age when they first came in season; some came in a month or two before they were two-year-olds and some much later. Eventually we only mated our fillies when they were well over two years old, well developed and came into season at a convenient time for our breeding plans. To let a filly breed too early benefits neither her nor her foal. She should be in good condition but not over fat.

A stallion should be fully able to take on limited stud duties as a three-year-old, and if he is a well developed and forward animal he can be allowed to give a few services earlier.

Though I have not had long enough experience in donkey breeding to say anything dogmatic about the number of services which a donkey stallion should give in a season, I feel I should say something about it. Some guidance may be obtained from a memorandum I have read on mule breeding, prepared for the government of India by Mr C.L. Sutherland.

The mule breeders appear to have regarded from fifty to seventy mares as sufficient for a normal jackass in a season, and up to one hundred for an especially well-fed and well-managed animal. Usually, 'a haras (mule-farm) with say, eight jacks will often have a clientele of 600 mares'. Horse mares, however, are not so easily put in foal by jackasses as by their own species, and so the mule breeder allows for the fact that some of them will need to be served several times before getting in foal. The memorandum lays down, as a general rule, that not more than two services per day (one in the morning and one in the evening) should be permitted to an established stallion specially maintained for stud purposes. Although excessive use of his sexual powers will not necessarily shorten his life, it will lessen his fertility. (The reader will appreciate that these figures relate to a hot country in which the ass is indigenous.) Finally, it mentions that the jackass should remain at home for service, rather than be taken round the country. This was of interest to us, for we found that on the rare occasions when we took a stallion elsewhere to give service it did not prove fruitful.

Moving on through the summer, August, being the peak month for holiday visitors, kept us busy too, with a welcome quota of interested callers.

Come September, if the weather was fine and cool, there was the unpleasant task of gelding the colt foals that one did not think suitable for stallions. This is a job our vet advocated for spring or early autumn when the weather is milder and there is less trouble from flies. We had our foals operated on at ages six weeks old to five months old, provided the vet thought it advisable at the time, otherwise we waited until the following spring. They were given a general anaesthetic in an open field on a suitable day and when the operation was over those who were not yet weaned went back to their mothers, who remained nearby, and were feeding again in a short while. The others rejoined their companions and it seemed to take a little longer before they too were feeding. For the next few days we kept them under supervision, just in case of infection or bleeding.

October ushered in weaning time, the most upsetting period of the year for all concerned, our only consolation then being that at least the young and the old had each other for company when mares and foals were separated. Weaning should take place when the foal is five to six months old. If the foal is strong and healthy and the mare is in foal again it can be weaned early. If, on the other hand, the foal is not over strong, it is better to leave it longer with the mare unless she seems out of condition herself. As is mentioned elsewhere, when separating the foal from the mare, the foal must be removed to a place out of earshot of her. For a few days the mare's udder will be swollen and tender before she eventually dries off. Both mare and foal should then be dosed against worms.

Before the year closed our young stock would be sold and departed to their new homes, leaving us with many fond memories and the hopes of a happy future for them.

7. *As a Pet*

SINCE WE HAD SPENT so much of our time
during the first few years of the stud with donkeys—in fact during the summer months we
seemed to live among them—I find it increasingly difficult to think why it took us all so long, as animal
lovers, to discover what a truly delightful, affectionate and interesting pet this undemanding little animal
could be.

Anyone who thinks that donkeys are stupid animals must, I am sure, never have had anything to do
with them or else be a very undiscerning person, as
they are without doubt intelligent, very knowing and
possess not only the proverbial sixth sense but, I feel
sure, even a seventh one. Some say they are obstinate,
but who likes to be pushed around, anyway? And
who goes more quietly and willingly when asked
politely than the well-trained ass? Surely if he had not
been supplied by nature with a generous fund of good
qualities, the manner in which he has been treated

over the years would have exhausted them all by now. Seldom do excessive ill-treatment, neglect and derision bring out the best qualities in either man or beast, and how frequently is contempt the only reward extended to those that serve too well and too cheaply.

So often compared to the horse and expected to have his attributes, one is inclined to forget that an ass is born an ass, not a horse. The qualities of his nature are numerous, and when disciplined, educated and generally cared for, he more than repays his bene-factor in kind. To those who are in the happy position of being able to accommodate them there is the great advantage that they live much longer than either dogs or cats, so one does not have to go through the agony of losing a beloved pet so often in a lifetime.

The reader may say that donkeys are not as com-panionable as dogs, because you cannot bring them into the house. Well, admittedly they cannot have the same run of the place that dogs have, but if your yard or driveway is easily accessible to your living quarters you will find that like us, they pop in an open door or push their heads through an open window (they are very careful and observant with glass), demanding and giving the same attentions as dogs. The foals, once used to it, trotted in and out of the house and, except for leaving hoof marks if it was dirty outside, were naturally house-trained and never messed inside.

Donkeys are full of curiosity and quickly assimilate the tempo of life going on around them. If an exces-sively shy animal was added to our equine family, we brought it up to the small paddock in front of the house to join some intimate friends. Remaining pretty standoffish for the first few days, it would quickly discard its distant attitude and become one of us. As our dogs used to bound about the place, barking and playing amongst them, and as plenty of activity in general went on all around, they soon got used to the hustle and bustle of life and lost their nervousness. I personally feel that much of donkeys' timidity is due to the excessively good hearing occasioned by their long ears and to the fact that their sight is not so good by comparison.

Donkeys are very distrustful of strange dogs; in fact they do not like them at all and will attack them with a quick up and down slicing movement of a foreleg, which can be very dangerous.

Darwin maintains that donkeys are not partial to water and that they will not even cross a brook, yet in a 1960s TV film made in Bulgaria many of them were shown swimming in a stream, and in Morocco during the rains they will ford streams up to their bellies and nearly every year cases occur when the animals are swept off their feet and both animal and rider are drowned. However, in my experience I found that even when leading them over a drain in a field that had water in it, they would often jib and refuse to jump it, but if the drain was dry they would go over easily.

One of their favourite pastimes is rolling and they purposely choose the most dirty, dusty and gritty place they can find. In fact, when they are in a field over a period of time, they make a special rolling patch. Perhaps this is done as a reproof to us for not grooming and caring for them as we should. It is surprising what a good grooming will do for them, especially in the spring or early summer when they are coating and look as though they are wearing a handed-down coat from a much older and larger relative. We used a wire brush about 2¼" x 4½" with a short handle and it really did the job happily for donkey and owner. About two eggcups full of linseed oil in a bran mash now and again helps them to discard their winter coat more quickly.

Perhaps if I lived inland and labour was no object, I should have been tempted to clip our trap donkey, as with polished harness and a shining, newly painted trap it would have been a really smart sight, though not giving us more enjoyment than we already had with our woolly pet, Alana, in her trap with the wobbly wheel. Such tranquillity on a real summer's day, jogging down the bohereens, no hurry there and no hurry back; perhaps a picnic tea, if there were blackberries to pick, with Alana having her meal on the 'long acre' as she followed us leisurely along the blackberry trail; no effort required, no words necessary, an inward glow prevailed. The world is busy— we are all busy—but the quietly rhythmic trot of the donkey on a country lane can modulate the tempo of our thoughts and so infect our ways that suddenly we are less busy than we thought.

To those who would like to pursue their happiness in this manner, a word of warning so that you will not, like me (nearly) 'fall by the wayside'! Be sure when you buy a reputedly 'broken-in' donkey that the truth has been spoken. With the memory of happy childhood pony-trap days in mind, a cart and harness were purchased soon after the arrival of our first two donkeys. With intense excitement we harnessed the animal sold to us as 'broken-in' and attached her to the new cart, which was to serve us for both work and pleasure.

I was in too great a hurry to wait for either the seat or the back of the cart to be finished before taking delivery so, kneeling gingerly on a cushion on the floor, I started down the drive. All went well until I crossed into a bohereen opposite to our house, which went downhill. Perhaps our harness was not properly adjusted—I shall never know—but the cart must have touched the donkey somewhere on her rear end, for with a series of bucks and leaps that would have put a rodeo horse to shame, she careered down the lane, only being halted by two strong men one buck before depositing me on the wayside with, I am sure, more than my dignity injured!

Needless to say, it was her first introduction to any kind of cart. A properly trained gelding is the best animal for trapping, as a stallion is not suitable for this job and if mares are used, they are generally about to foal, or have a foal at foot, when needed in the summer months. It is easy to train a donkey with a little time and patience, and those interested will find instructions in at least two most interesting and helpful donkey books: *People with Long Ears* by Robin Borwick and *Donkeys* by M.R. de Wesselow.

The well-trained donkey really excels himself as a ride for young children. Unless 'oats fed', speed not being a speciality of these animals, they prefer to go at a leisurely and dignified gait that is perfect for the equestrian beginner. Even the most nervous child will soon acquire confidence on a well-trained donkey and so have many happy years with a pet, learning most of the essential points necessary for good horsemanship in later years. Many children ride them without saddles, but to be really comfortable a saddle and stirrups are required. We had a light, padded leather saddle that was ideal, being soft for child and donkey. I would also suggest a leather strap attached to the back of the saddle with a loop at the end of it, called a crupper, which goes around the animal's tail and so prevents the saddle from slipping onto its neck.

These, with the addition of a bridle and bit, will give years of service, especially if the young rider learns to care for them, too. As it takes many spills to make a good jockey, so it is said, a young rider may have his quota also. Though when he has travelled that short distance to land on the soft ground near his pet's legs, he will not be any more surprised than the donkey, who will look at him reproachfully with those all-seeing dark orbs, and allow the casualty to climb up under his tummy or between his legs to the position he once occupied to try again. I have seen this happen many times and wondered how many children who had lost their nerve early in life through falls from an over-enthusiastic pony could have been saved by our patient, well-trained donkey.

8. Donkey Life

A REMARK FROM Rev. Mahaffy's paper that the advent of the ass as a beast of burden in Ireland 'was gradual, therefore silent' has often returned to my mind. It is a remark so applicable to people of inward stature—though with a different demeanour on the outside—who have been around for a long time unnoticed and who, when eventually their true worth breaks through, are really noticed for the first time.

Could not this be applied to our worthy, gentle ass? Of all the countries that he has penetrated and resided in, I think the ass has found his spiritual home in Ireland, even to such an extent that most people think he is indigenous. H.V. Morton finds 'the cow, the pig and the donkey are the props of the Irish countryside', in his book *In Search of Ireland*.

It seems almost certain that the ass first became involved in the life of the Irish peasantry early in the nineteenth century, and developed an affinity with them. Perhaps it was an unconscious assumption of hardships shared and suffered, a oneness in the vague acceptance of the blows received from so-called friend or foe, that with a patience born of long suffering they have waited like their sorely tried masters of yesterday for the lessening of their burdens, which is now at last in sight. A donkey may be just a donkey to some people, but once you know them and they know that you know them, they will let you know that they know you, too. It may take time, if they have not been born into the family, and especially if they have not come from happy homes, but one quiet day as you browse among them listening to the melody of summer, or have withdrawn to a nearby bank to ponder what you will, you could be recalled from your reverie by a soft snuffling noise, the gentle nudge of a warm muzzle, or a sort of 'till death do us part' look from the owner of a pair of deep, dark eyes, who has detached herself from the 'madding crowd' to commune with you alone, and so with her there is no parting of the ways.

Not with all of them does one feel the same rapport, which is perhaps just as well and not to be encouraged when one deals in numbers, but with the chosen few there is no escape. Our few early losses in death were hard to bear, but we remembered them as a sacrifice to our education and tried to profit by it.

Our losses to buyers, too, were a trial, but one that had to be born with fortitude as it was inevitable; but, when you can feel as sure as it is possible to be that their prospective home will be a happy one, they must away. With that idea in its proper place at the back of your mind when the foaling season starts, your days can be interlaced with many joys. Most young animals are attractive to animal-lovers, but a playful donkey foal is completely enchanting and, I am sure, the greatest time-consumer ever born.

As the days pass by there is no mischief invented that he will not try his hand at, if given a chance. Often when only a few hours old the first buck is attempted. Once settled down to this serious business of living he can really start looking around and, after proper enquiries by mother to make sure that his contemporaries are 'nice people to know', peaceful co-existence reigns and life takes on its normal tenor in each individual way. So much of interest to a young fellow—strange noises, strange people and strange places all to be investigated.

If the day looks dull with no one around to give and receive attention, 'taking the mickey out of Ma' is always a favourite sport: nibbling at her all over, jumping at her and even turning his rear and laying into her tummy with his hind legs is not overlooked. It is astonishing what he can get away with, except at her feeding time, when many a box on the ears or the menacing lift of a hind leg is forthcoming.

Lying stretched full length on the grass in the sun amongst the buttercups is bliss and makes up for any boring days sheltering from wind and rain. Trying his paces is perhaps the most exhilarating pastime of all, especially if there is a younger newcomer to show off to, and it is quite amazing what speed can be obtained. The best fun of all, though, are the evening capers: superb trials of speed around the field with his friends, both at the full gallop and at the very special 'donkey trot', great bouncy strides, with nose pointed sharply upwards and slightly sideways. Around and around the paddock with astonishing speed and agility, in and out and over every obstacle in sight. Should there be an audience, he will hold his head especially high, and he won't always see a neighbour approaching at the same high speed. Such losses of dignity are rare and the capers continue with many indescribable antics, until Mother ushers him off to bed in the shelter.

Another day is born, a calm sunny one, and the paddock is littered with different coloured little bodies lying asleep, flat as pancakes, so somnolent that even if you walk among them, they are too drowsy to lift a head. If you go quietly up to one and lay your hand gently over his eye, he will not move until you lift it. Others will enjoy it if you sit beside them and do some scratching work, perhaps putting their head on your knees to make the work less arduous, leading in time to perhaps the whole fluffy bundle on your lap.

Life is not all idleness, though, and the foal must learn a little discipline, too. How to lead is an important lesson, and the earlier he is taught the better. In the first stage it is a great help to have someone who will walk behind to give appropriate encouragement with a small rod if necessary, while you lead him from the near side (left) by a light halter made of narrow webbing. He will soon learn and if you move your mares and foals around from one field to another, lead the foals, as the mares will follow. To start with it is easiest to find a foal who is a little apart from his mother and lead him up to her, providing you know the right mother, because the foal is not always sure. One season we had two nearly black foals born within a few hours of each other in the same field. For the first day or two the mothers, who had been great friends, made unfriendly grimaces at each other when they met, which was quite often, as the two foals were friendly. Very soon, though, they all settled down to communal living with the foals drinking from whichever 'mum' was handy.

Generally it is the foals who will approach the 'milk bar' first, without prompting, but not always. One delightful mare we had called Breaffy always reminded her offspring when it was mealtime. If they happened to be sitting down, well, it was time they arose, so, gently but firmly, she gripped the foal on the neck with her mouth and lifted it up to feed.

Donkeys have so many entertaining habits that it is hard to recount them all. It is amusing to see that when one calls them from the other side of a field they will wind their way across, single file, keeping on a hardly discernible grass pathway. If they were bunched at the gateway when I came to call, I was greeted by a multitude of snuffly, squeaky noises, which I am sure, if recorded, would only be recognized by donkey folk. Mares seldom bray except when in season, very hungry, in distress or in greeting. Stallions can be noisy fellows, especially in the mating season. Each individual tone of bray is recognizable. One mare we had called Easter had a real falsetto tone, and our white stallion, Canavaun (Irish for bog-cotton), seemed to include every note on the 'donkey scale'. When foals bray they make a mixture of amusing sounds, too varied to describe.

We had one lady called Rainbow who was very fond of her grub and, if she happened to be in the front paddock during the winter months, watched our windows in the morning to see when the blinds were drawn back, acknowledging the action by a loud request for breakfast.

Keeping track of such a large number of donkeys could be difficult if one did not have a naming system. So we started by calling our mares names that could be followed up by an associate name, such as Gentian, whose foal was then called after another wild flower, Orchis. Norina from *Don Pasquale* led the operatic list; Jig led the dancers; Fanchea, being the daughter of an erstwhile king of Munster, kept royalty in the picture. Luck Penny, though taking care of the lineage of coins, had a special significance to Irish people, as after a private deal has been made, the vendor always gives back a small sum of money to the purchaser for luck. So our theme of names helped to keep us in order until, for some unremembered reason, we developed a 'miscellaneous' line, which took quite a lot of negotiating not to tangle up with the others.

So our donkey life proceeded with a new interest each day; perhaps a new foal in the morning, who by the evening was moving about the paddock with those funny little jerky movements that they retain for days. Visiting mares to be mated arrived at all hours from local places, and from many counties of Ireland, in all sorts of vehicles—lorries, tractors, trailers, led from a bicycle and even harnessed to a cart—to which they would be united again after the service.

Interested visitors came to see the donkeys and foals from many countries, often bringing useful information of *Equus asinus* from their homelands, one and all rapturizing on the unspoilt beauty of our rugged and colourful coast at Spanish Point.

There were days of haymaking, filling up the barns, thatching and tying down the large trams of hay near the shelters to withstand the winter gales. We had evenings of sunsets, unbelievably lovely, that must beggar the skill of the world's greatest writers and painters to describe, when the animals, like us all, felt the magic of it, ceased their play and lay rapt in the glow. Quiet, moonlit nights, with the constant melody of a calm sea and, outside my window, the noise of lightly pounding hoofs, drew us to lift the curtain on the nocturnal frolics of both mares and foals, who relish the moonlight hours. Other days and nights the sea and the wind argued madly, the rain lashing them both; on others a calm, mist hovered around, all making the pattern of life in County Clare one that we had no wish to change.

County Clare has something of everything that is Irish. Both the past and the present meet with understanding and joy. Her gifts are manifold and she bestows them radiantly on all who love her. Perhaps one of her charms, less obvious than others, is her numerous bohereens, ambling along from the highways to nearly forgotten, and legendary places. Dia dhuit County Clare.

9. Care

WHEN STARTING OFF on any project in life it is important to find out as much information as possible about it first, but finding out data on the care and breeding of donkeys, especially in the moody climate of the west of Ireland, was not an easy job. This was mainly because so little value has been put on donkeys in Ireland that few have bothered with their troubles, and the ones who did could not afford to give them the necessary care and attentions.

Donkeys have the reputation of being hardy animals, and there is no doubt that once they have reached maturity they are, but in their early life they have more enemies than anyone who is only slightly acquainted with them could suspect. It was astonishing that in the 1960s edition of the *Chemist Veterinary Handbook*, they were denied a chapter among all the domestic animals catered for (which included goats, rabbits and even bees) and were only referred

to a few times in the chapter on horses. Now that situation has been remedied in that one can purchase a
specialist work entitled *The Professional Handbook
of the Donkey*, compiled by Dr Elisabeth D. Svendsen.

They have certain traits of the horse and pony, so
that some knowledge of these animals can be a great
help in the care of donkeys, but their own special
peculiarities are only revealed to those who are interested enough to study them by constant observation
and contact with them in varied surroundings. Their
troubles are at last being recognized, though treatment for some of them is still in its experimental
stages, so any information collected by interested persons could be of great help in ascertaining the causes
of unusual maladies.

Our first years with our new family taught us
many lessons, some of them painful ones and never to
be forgotten, but teaching us at the same time some
of the *do*s and *don't*s of what is necessary for happy
donkey life. When dealing in large numbers, as we
were, conditions are apt to be more pronounced,
though it is as well to remember that individuals suffering in a minor way could pass unnoticed. Because
these animals are not good fighters when they are ill,
it is absolutely necessary to visit one's stock regularly
and, with young foals, twice a day is not too much,
especially if weather conditions are bad. This is a case
where the saying that 'a stitch in time saves nine' is
really applicable, because when they are ill, which I
am happy to say is not often, they need immediate

and constant attention until they have recovered.

Until recently donkeys were seldom kept in herds in Ireland, and in none of the cases that I have heard about in the past have they prospered. Rev. J.P. Mahaffy gives us this information in 1917:

> The experiment was made about 60 years ago by a Mr Hassard, who owned a rough heather mountain in County Antrim, of letting asses loose to live there as do the rough ponies of the country. They all died out in a couple of years, this proving what Aristotle said long ago; that asses will not live wild in a cold country.

Added to this I have been informed personally by a man in County Galway that he gave a small herd (under a dozen animals), which he had bought as travelling companions for the horses he exported, the run of about 500 acres of land and, having a large number of animals to care for, paid little heed to the asses, who died off in a short while. These two instances, I think, are enough to show that they need reasonable attention. Any definite indication that the animals are ill necessitates the calling in of one's vet immediately, but there are certain things that can be done to keep them healthy and contented, and other things that can be done while waiting for the vet to arrive.

Where you live will have a certain amount to do with the troubles you may have. One of the little troubles that is prevalent among donkeys almost everywhere is WORMS, and if these are not taken care of, they can turn into big troubles. Those owners who have few donkeys, some cattle and plenty of appetizing grassland do not have as much to worry about as those who have a large herd, no cattle and not as much grassland as they would like. The reason is that over-stocking and permanent pastures are the chief causes of worm infestation. With sufficient land those who have cattle can alternate the use of their fields with them, thereby reducing the risk that the life cycle of the worms will be completed, because the life of a worm demands that it spend part of its time in the host animal and part in the field.

An animal that is kept in a stable is not as liable to be infested by them, but then donkeys are seldom kept there unless they are ill. Since we had a large herd of animals, and many visiting ones, we took the precaution of worming them about every three months. When we bought a new donkey we wormed it immediately, and again two weeks afterwards, to kill the worms that would have hatched out in the meantime; worming then continued at three-monthly intervals. When a donkey is heavily infested with worms it will look in bad condition, sometimes scouring persistently, rubbing his rear on the gate post or railings, or even coughing. A pot-bellied animal is also a suspect.

We administered the worm dose in a feed of oats and bran or, if the patient would not oblige by taking it that way, by drench. This is done by diluting the worm dose in some water and putting it in a bottle, the size of which depends on the dose to be administered as prescribed by the vet. I used a small plastic bottle obtainable at a chemist for the younger animals and a large glass bottle for the older ones. It is necessary to have someone to help who will hold the donkey's head up while you administer the dose by inserting the neck of the bottle into the side of its mouth where there are no teeth. Then pour in a small quantity at a time and allow the donkey to swallow comfortably. Some animals are co-operative and some definitely are not. For these latter ones your assistant will need to stroke the throat gently to encourage it to swallow. At the slightest sign of coughing or choking you must let the animal's head down immediately. It was not my favourite pastime, but a very necessary one if one's donkey family is to thrive. A word of warning, however, must be given to the uninitiated about 'drenching': it is possible to choke the animal, so get your vet, or some experienced person, to show you exactly how to do it before you attempt it yourself, because it is easy to let the liquid go down the wrong way with disastrous results, if you do not know how to avoid it.

As well as these more prevalent worms, there are other worm enemies to look out for, such as LUNG-WORM. This is to be found in donkeys much more than is appreciated. On our farm it was the same species that is found in horses, but not the same as in cattle. We found the medicines used for cattle proved reasonably successful in treating our donkeys. The symptoms are coughing and a loss of condition which, if not treated, could be followed by pneumonia and maybe death. The few cases we had were mostly in young stock less than a year old and all recovered after treatment.

So you can see that worms seem to be the donkey's public enemy number one, an enemy that should not be underrated and must be kept at bay.

FLUKE is another disease that can be found in donkeys. It is caused by liver fluke and the symptoms are also a lack of condition and a staring coat. The fluke, during its life cycle, must enter a snail and leave it again to be effective and as this snail is prevalent in marshy, muddy places, wet land should be drained and the ditches kept clean and open. If either of these troubles is suspected, samples of droppings (faeces) should be given to your vet for analysis.

In my experience scouring in young foals calls for prompt observation. It may only be an indication that the mare is coming in season and, if you think that that is so, there is nothing to worry about. However, it could be a sign of other things, too, such as a chill or an infection which, if not seen to at once, could cause big trouble, so it pays to give it careful attention. If the foal continues scouring and is unusually quiet and listless, call your vet at once. Since these young animals naturally lack the resistance of older ones, they require immediate attention. The vet may be unavoidably delayed, so the foal must be stabled and kept warm. If looking very poorly it can be given an eggcup full of brandy mixed with a little water and as much attention as possible, as of all animals I have had anything to do with—and I was brought up on a farm—the donkey requires the most nursing and encouragement when ill.

COLIC is a term applied to abdominal pains, which could be caused by indigestion through a complete change of feeding, or other dietetic errors such as over-eating newly cut grass, or a poisonous herb. The symptoms are obvious distress and the animal may paw the ground, even getting down and rolling and drawing its legs to its belly in pain. This again is where your vet must be called as soon as possible.

It can happen that mares will abort their foals about halfway through their pregnancy: this could either be due to the fact that they were in bad condition, or it could be caused by an infection. A few of our mares did this and all went on to breed healthy foals.

It would indeed be strange if one had any kind of animal family without a spot of trouble occasionally but, I repeat, regular visiting will result in that 'stitch in time'.

Perhaps I should add a word about things that are POISONOUS to donkeys. Remember they are vegetarians, and anything made of meat or fish is poisonous to them, so while they will enjoy your bread they will be very ill if they consume your meat or fish sandwiches. So far as vegetation is concerned their own instincts will provide a pretty good guide as to what they should avoid, but there are some things that appear tempting to them even though poisonous. I would particularly mention the leaves of the yew tree or bush, and beware of all evergreens in quantity. Laburnum leaves and seeds are also poisonous. Lead is another lethal substance and should not be used for drinking or feeding troughs.

It is useful sometimes to feed lawn-mowings, but they should be spread lightly over the ground, and never put in a heap lest they ferment and cause indigestion.

10. *And More Care*

Uncared-for hooves have been a great cause for complaint from overseas visitors to Ireland—a complaint only too often warranted. Donkey's hooves grow quickly, and therefore need frequent paring and, as many country people who own a donkey live far away from a blacksmith, it is not always easy for them to get their animals done regularly if they do not use them for transport. The owners of donkeys that are used in transport, however, have no such excuse, as there is sure to be a blacksmith within range of their journey. If your animal is to be used regularly on the road it should be shod completely, but for occasional work it is sufficient to shoe the front feet, otherwise the hooves should be pared every six or seven weeks, allowing for individual growth.

Hoof-attention for our herd was quite a business, but we had a programme and kept to it, weather and other unexpected circumstances permitting. Few donkeys mind this job, especially when they are cared for in this respect while young and manageable. Again, there are the exceptions, and we owned one of them. A seven-year-old mare purchased on request from a man who was going blind turned out to be a terror for the blacksmith, so much so that he had to 'throw her' to pare her hooves. This was done expertly and quickly with a rope without any injury to the animal, except to her dignity. When thrown, her four legs were tied together and she had to remain on her back until the job is done.

A folding hoof-pick is easily carried in the pocket when visiting your stock. Even if its application is not always necessary, the frequent lifting of their legs to inspect the hooves will accustom the donkey to this kind of attention and facilitate handling if ailments should occur.

One of these ailments could be LAMINITIS, a disease of the foot in which the sensitive laminae immediately under the horny wall of the hoof are inflamed or congested. It is a serious complaint and should be attended to at once as it is also a most painful one, akin to an abscess under a fingernail.

If your animal is very lame without visible cuts and swellings on his legs, or hoof injuries, but is abnormally hot and tender above his hoof (the coronet) and obviously suffering, it is more than likely that he has fever in his hoof.

While you are waiting for the vet to arrive, the offending foot or feet should be poulticed. A bran poultice consisting of sufficient bran to cover the foot, and a tablespoon of salt as an antiseptic, in boiling water (I pop in a little linseed oil for good measure) is easily prepared. While this is cooling, tie a light flannel bandage around the pastern (just above the coronet), then pour the mixture onto strong cloths or sacking and fix the poultice around the hoof and tie it together over the bandage, which will prevent the leg from being rubbed. Over the poultice a plastic bag will keep in the moisture and heat, which helps the hoof to expand and relieves the pressure within. Another bandage over the ends of the cloth or sacking to help keep them in place should make it a first-class job. Then be sure your donkey is standing on soft ground either inside or outside and produce another bran mash, this time for internal comfort.

Three of our donkeys had laminitis and each in their hind legs. This is not without interest as in horses, I believe, it is more common for the forelegs to be affected.

According to various sources of information, the reason for this complaint is said to be over-rich feeding, worms, overwork or excessive galloping on hard ground when out of condition. Animals are also said to develop it after a bad attack of colic, heavy doses of physic, congestion of the vascular system from consuming large quantities of cold water and food while over-heated or, in the case of mares, when very heavily in foal. I found it hard to ascertain what caused the complaint in our own three victims, but I suspected overfeeding due to constant greedy shoving and pushing for the lion's share of grub to have been the downfall of at least one of our animals, and a great heaviness in foal could have produced it in another.

Forgetting the 'in betweens' of the donkey for the moment we rise rapidly from his hooves to view his TEETH. Frequent inspection of these should not be overlooked if the animal seems in bad condition, as there are times, however remote, when his teeth require attention.

Far back in his jaws are the molars, the grinding teeth, and these can sometimes give trouble. Because the upper jaw is wider than the lower one and the grinding movement is from side to side, the teeth on the outer edges of the upper jaw and on the inner edges of the lower jaw do not get any wear. This in time may cause sharp points to develop, which could lacerate the cheeks and tongue, hampering mastication and causing digestive troubles if not observed and cared for by filing with a tooth rasp. This is another job for your vet or an experienced person, if your donkey is not to run the risk of having his tongue rasped as well as his teeth.

At birth the donkey foal has no teeth, although the front ones are sometimes visible under the gums. Very soon the first eight milk teeth appear, followed six to nine months later by four more. These twelve teeth are the central, lateral and corner incisors, the biting teeth, which eventually fall out to make room for the

WITHDRAWN

twelve permanent incisors. From about the age of two-and-a-half years onwards these milk teeth will be discarded, starting with the central incisors, followed by the lateral and corner ones, to be replaced by the permanent teeth in the same order, until, at five years old or thereabouts he has a full mouth.

Until then, it is relatively easy to tell his age, but from five onwards experience, through constant observation, is the best instructor, as there is much to learn about the markings, shape and length of the teeth. Frequently the first lesson is to differentiate between the milk and permanent teeth, by remembering that the milk teeth are smaller and whiter than the permanent ones.

When the male donkey is four years old he will produce four tusk-like teeth, a little way behind his incisors, called tushes. These do not seem to be of much use to him, which is perhaps why the canny female invariably exists without them!

Now, a female who can cause a lot of extra work in your establishment—the mare who is SHORT OF MILK. So be sure when making the daily rounds to satisfy yourself that your mare is all right in that respect. If the mare's udder looks very light and the foal keeps going back to feed frequently with tugging movements, it is a sign that he is not getting enough. Perhaps a change to better pasturage with not too much clover in it, which donkeys do not care for, will help. If not, consult your vet. If at any time it should happen that the mare's udder is swollen and hot, then you should call your vet immediately. As milk is life to the young foal, it is vital that all goes well in that direction. It usually does, but in the unusual case supplementary feeding is necessary.

Only once did we have anxiety over shortage of milk and luckily the foal was three or four months old, but as he caught a chill in late autumn we helped him on through the winter with a bottle, to his great advantage, using a baby food mixture, glucose and some Ribena.

Once again we experienced another difficulty in feeding with a small foal and an oddly shaped mare. Mum was very stout low down in the tummy and the foal, having been born in the evening in rather a rough part of the field, was too tired after the extra exertion of trying to stand on the bumpy surface to make an adequate effort at feeding. It necessitated bringing both mare and foal to the stable and some patient work by a neighbouring vet before eventually mare and foal met in the right places. Altogether an unusual occurrence, but because the trouble was observed, help was available.

CONSTIPATION is also something to be vigilant about, especially if your animal seems off-colour. As a lubricant, liquid paraffin can safely be given to both foals and adults. If an aperient is required, two tablespoons of Epsom salts in a bran mash or a dose of castor oil can be given to adult donkeys. If no result is noticed from these treatments after a reasonable period, you must consult your vet.

During one excessively warm and dry summer a seven-week-old filly of ours appeared slightly gaunt and listless. We immediately called in our vet who suspected an internal blockage. After five sad days she died, having made a gallant fight for existence helped by every possible attention. The autopsy revealed a block of dry dung of fibrous material that oral medicine had failed to disperse and that was too high up the bowel for an enema to affect.

I came across a similar case soon afterwards and wondered as a layperson whether it could have been caused by the unusually moistureless texture of our herbage on such small digestions.

A COUGH is a disturbing complaint for both donkey and owner, physically for the donkey and mentally for the owner until he can discover the cause of it and effect a cure.

As mentioned previously, animals heavily infested with worms will cough, and continuous coughing could mean a lungworm infection. Again it may be due to a chill from exposure, sudden changes in temperature or a draughty or badly ventilated stable, and if not attended to quickly could develop into bronchitis or pneumonia. Also there is the cough that comes from a passing irritant in the throat or from indigestion; this is a short, hard, dry-sounding cough not like the longer softer one issuing from the animal with the previously mentioned complaints.

You should always take notice of any coughing in your donkey and, unless you are satisfied that it is of a temporary variety, the sooner the better for your vet to come and investigate the matter. Meanwhile keep the patient in an airy stable, cosily wrapped up, and feed a warm bran mash, as you should also do if he has caught a CHILL and is shivering, with icy cold ears and running from his nose and eyes, even scouring; as care now can prevent the chill developing into a more serious malady. If at any time your animal has a thick yellowish discharge from his nostrils and is coughing, do not omit to search high up under his jaw to see if he has swollen glands. Should they be discovered you can suspect STRANGLES, and as this is a highly contagious disease the vet's advice and attention will again be in demand.

Although RINGWORM rarely occurs in donkeys, I feel it should be referred to here because it is also highly contagious. A disease of the skin caused by a fungus, it is recognizable by raised circular patches of hair through which exude a small amount of fluid; the hairs then stick together and eventually fall out, leaving greyish-white crusty or scaly patches of skin. Even with medical advice, meticulous care will be required to prevent the disease from spreading.

Donkeys are subject to annoyances such as warts, lice, various skin eruptions, cuts and abrasions. Your vet will remove the warts for you, and there are many louse powders available to rub on the donkeys' coats to get rid of lice, which should be repeated at intervals until the coat is cleared of them. No donkey with lice will thrive. Skin eruptions are mostly due to dietary errors, such as over-rich feeding, or the eating of certain herbs that produce an allergy. These can often be eliminated by ordinary observation and care and the occasional dose of Epsom salts in a feed, but your vet must be consulted if these eruptions continue or unaccountable lumps or swellings appear: donkeys do get tumours and other growths that need his attention. Unless they are serious and require stitching, slight cuts and abrasions can be cleaned with salt and water. An aerosol antiseptic spray can help to keep them clean and heal them, especially if it also contains a fly repellent.

We noticed that most of our white and broken-coloured animals tended to get raw or crusty muzzles at times and that Vaseline, glycerine, olive or castor oil slightly warmed, coped adequately with the trouble. Many Irish donkeys get unsightly looking skin on their ears from excessive wet, but it rights itself when finer weather comes.

It is a help to have some articles together in a special place for times of need and those included in the following list are useful and practical:

A rug and canvas girth with pads that go either side of the backbone over the rug to keep both from slipping.

Two bottles with long necks for drenching: a small plastic one and a larger one like a Ribena bottle.

A baby's bottle and some black teats that resemble the mare's teat.

Cotton wool, bandages and some pieces of heavy cloth or sacking for poulticing.

Disinfectant in liquid and spray form. Liquid paraffin. Epsom salts. Vaseline. Healing ointment. Louse powder. A tube of eye ointment. Glucose. A small tot of brandy. Surgical scissors.

Some sterilized gut. Animal embrocation. A veterinary thermometer (in case your vet should lose his on a dark and stormy night—beg your pardon, vet!). Only an experienced person should attempt to take the donkey's temperature, as the thermometer has to be inserted gently into the rectum and could easily get broken in the process. It should read 100.4°F in normal health.

A strong disinfectant is also advisable for the stable, which should be thoroughly cleaned and disinfected after each occupant. If a few bags of turf-dust or sawdust are easily obtainable they are better on the stable floor than straw when a new foal is in residence, as it makes walking less arduous for him.

Anyone with a small well-fenced plot of land can keep a donkey, but if you wish to reward him for the affection and unremitting enjoyment he will give, you must see that he is cared for. Having observed their habits closely, I would put shelter from bad weather, one-half to three-quarters of a ton of hay in winter, depending on where you live and the length of the winter, clean fresh water and companionship, human or otherwise, as essentials merited by any self-respecting donkey.

They are exceptionally sociable animals, thriving on attention, even having their own special chums among the herd. For those who can manage it, I would always advocate keeping two at least, as a solitary animal without interests, like a solitary human without interests, tends to become dull and despondent.

I hope that having read this account of troubles that might occur, the reader will not be deterred from keeping one or more of these most loveable and entertaining animals, remembering that horses and dogs suffer from maladies galore at times, and are yet our most popular and numerous pleasure-producing animals.

It is always tempting to spoil the object of one's affections. Now and again, this is certainly permissible and especially after an illness. For an animal that requires extra nourishment I heartily recommend a bowl of porridge. A few handfuls of oatmeal, soaked in cold water until it attains a soft consistency, can be eaten with a large pinch of salt standing up, as is done by our neighbour the Scotsman.

11. Decisions

WHEN ONE HAS MADE the decision to embark on breeding donkeys, it is a good idea to decide as early on as possible what kind of donkey to specialize in. This may seem a strange remark, as at one time a donkey was just a donkey.

Nevertheless, times have changed and the market is open to a greater variety of shapes, sizes and colourings than ever before. Ireland, unfortunately, allowed herself to lag behind in the realization of their potentialities as pets, both for children and grown-ups, and in permitting them their rightful place in the show ring like most other domestic animals.

In England at the start of the seventies, an organization was formed for people interested in donkeys called the Donkey Show Society. One of the many useful and interesting objects of this society is the drawing up of a list setting out the conformation and points of the donkey for show purposes. While not everyone may agree with all of these points, there must be some criteria to judge by and this list seems excellent.

If I could have added to it I would. The variety of donkey with a shorter and wider head alone seems to have been considered as yet, but in fact there are other clear types. One in particular I would include is the variety of donkey that is reminiscent of an Arab pony, with a longer head, finely chiselled and tapering to the nostrils—a very attractive variety.

As for breeders who wish to sell their stock for pets, they need not concentrate so much on conformation as on temperament and on the general characteristics that make the donkeys suitable for constant handling and petting. With very few exceptions donkeys love attention, though some more so than others, and it is a rule without exception that a placid and friendly mare promotes the same attributes in her offspring. So if you wish to breed pets, a really gentle, amicable mare is a great help to begin with.

Another opening for the breeder is the donkey used for giving children rides on beaches, at fêtes and other places of entertainment, where conformation is not the major point, but where a sturdy and well-trained animal is essential. Anyone who breeds for this purpose should make it their business to be sure their stock is sold to buyers of good repute in the care of them during this more arduous way of life. It is nice to know that the RSPCA have an excellent set of rules covering the hire of donkeys at seaside and other resorts, which have now been widely adopted by the ISPCA.

Donkey derbies have become increasingly popular, though the breeding of animals for this sport should be approached with some reservations. To partake regularly and successfully in a derby calls for strongly made, swift-footed, 'oats-fed' asses and, though there is nothing to criticize in the breeding and feeding of them as such, there seems much to criticize in the derbies themselves. If one could feel that the races were always held under proper supervision, and humane treatment was assured, it would then undoubtedly be a great incentive to breeders to cater for this remunerative sport, which could be enjoyed by many. Racing donkeys with deformed, uncared-for hooves on roads and prodding with penknives and other sharp instruments should be among the main things to be prohibited.

Specializing in colour is another choice open to breeders. This can be a fascinating occupation and is one that we were most interested in at our stud. People who are limited to the number of animals they can keep may want to specialize in trying to breed just one colour. How encouraging if, in the not too distant future, every show in Ireland would have classes for donkeys that include a class for individual colours incorporating conformation. What a diversity of donkey colours and shades there are to choose from, so many that it is hard to find names for them all because of the amalgamation of the various species that has taken place over the years. What a challenge to segregate certain colours by specialized breeding, with conformation in mind, and thereby produce the thoroughbreds of each particular branch of colouring.

In spite of the fact that so many donkeys have been exported to England, most Irish owners have always kept a 'good ass'. So let us remember we still have plenty of beautiful animals and can partake successfully in breeding for all these various interests.

Prior to 1970 transport abroad had been a major problem for young, better-class stock, but thanks to a co-operative and far-seeing transport company it became possible to fly both young and fully grown stock under excellent conditions to many countries.

Donkeys are not good travellers by sea, the main reason being that they cannot be seasick, though they suffer the pangs of sickness. When distressed they lose condition quickly and the stories that have reached me about the rigours of their journeys crossing the sea, especially in inclement weather, make me very grateful that it is not now necessary to subject them to this ordeal. We sent them to England and Scotland by air in light wooden crates, with two animals to a crate as they travel much more happily and less nervously together.

Having trained them to go in and out of the trailer and got them used to standing quietly in it for longish periods, we then took them early to the airport to get them used to the excessive noise of the planes. While we were waiting, there was always a patch of grass to nibble at, or we brought some hay if the day was wet. Once they had got used to the airport bustle they went quietly into their crate, commanding the VIP attention they feel is their due and arriving at their destination in excellent condition.

A word of warning to those who are sending an animal on a long journey; make sure that it has room in the crate or box to stale. This means that the donkeys must have sufficient space in which to stretch out their hind legs, as otherwise they do not seem able to stale.

The size of the crate for air travel is, however, limited, so they should be restricted to it for the minimum time. Arrangements must be made for them to be taken out of the crate in between flights whenever possible.

For those who are contemplating the purchase of a donkey trailer the following information may prove helpful. Some laths screwed to the floor of the trailer and ramp enable the animals to keep their foothold. The internal measurements of our trailer were: length 85", width 43", height 53" at the sides and 59" to top of the rounded roof. The back wall of the trailer that let down to make a ramp was 46". Though I do not remember how we arrived at such odd figures we found the results to be extremely practical and it accommodated two average-size adult donkeys or three or four youngsters in comfort.

Two generally travel best when one is facing forwards and the other backwards, frequently steadying themselves by each resting its head on the other's back. We had no division in our trailer, so single occupants generally travelled diagonally with their quarters in a corner. Protective padding prevented sores due to rubbing. A window along the front of the trailer allowed us to keep an eye on them from the car, while a strip along each of the sides was detachable to allow for extra ventilation. Attention to such detail went a long way towards preventing distress in travel.

A shocking instance showing lack of understanding of the rigours due to confined space on a journey is recounted by George Moore in *Hail and Farewell*. Two gentlemen at the beginning of the last century thought to improve the breed of asses in Ireland by importing sire asses from Egypt, which they had purchased for between £75 and £100 each, at that time half the price of the large Spanish sires. Seventeen of these 'beautiful little animals, alert as flies' trotted and cantered along the docks to the ship where, alas, a sad fate awaited them. Although every ass had a stall to himself, the bars so carefully erected around them for their safety against mutual kicking and biting prevented them from stretching in order to stale, with the appalling result that they died from burst bladders. When the boat reached Malta seven remained alive and, after delay caused by mechanical breakdown, only one of these survived to be landed at Marseilles, 'a forlorn and decrepit scarecrow ass' who, when he eventually arrived in Ireland, would not so much as look at the pretty white, black and brown asses from Kerry assembled for the purpose of having their breed improved. Perhaps the most incredible part of this incident is that the grooms who travelled with them appear to have attached no importance to their failure to stale.

While on the subject of travelling, we were surprised by the number of people who travelled very long distances with a mare to one of our stallions, and yet left her foal at home, even when very young indeed. Such long hours without its mother's milk, or the reassurance of her presence, must be distressing for the foal, and a cause of discomfort and anxiety to the mare. With a little care foals can be brought as well quite easily, and it is better that they should.

Yet another road open for the donkey breeder to venture forth on is the 'open road'. Pack-asses, gaily decorated, carrying the tents and other equipment of erstwhile heavily laden hikers, could become a popular national tourist attraction. Our countryside has many beautiful byways and what better ways for energetic youth or satiated city folk to capture the peace and tranquillity of rural Ireland than in the company of our leisurely paced friend?

We have already seen two Swedish boys along the road in the company of a staid and dignified, though heavily laden, quadruped and from the up-to-date news bulletins the companionship prospers happily. Providing we now breed an adequate supply for our home interests, and take what opportunities we can to improve our stock, what is there to stop us from making donkeys an important and valuable export? Perhaps the Bloodstock and Breeders' Association will eventually allow this breed of equines to have a place in their registers, making the old horse copers' saying 'sure isn't an ounce of breedin' worth a ton of feedin'?' applicable to the Irish ass.

Donkeys may be used in the field of therapeutics: it has been found that the use of a pony as a pet has been very helpful to certain types of learning disabled or maladjusted children. Those who are normally unable to communicate with humans will talk to and caress a pony. If this is so with ponies, why should it not be so with donkeys, which are quieter and more manageable for nervous children, and less expensive to acquire?

After our stud had been in operation for a few years we were privileged to be able to donate pairs of selected animals, which had been prepared by us, to several hospitals, homes, and societies in Ireland that care especially for both physically and mentally disabled children. Our Lady's Hospital in Ennis, County Clare, under the direction of Dr Patrick Power, became the first hospital in the country to countenance keeping donkeys for the benefit of its patients.

From the feedback we received we learned how donkey riding gave the children a great deal of pleasure. They made vital contact with the donkeys, which they were often unable to experience with people, and were rewarded with satisfaction instead of frustration.

In this fashion it gave the children the opportunity of participating in a normal play activity that they could not otherwise have experienced and enjoyed. Apart from the remedial value, the results from riding in terms of pleasure and personal achievement were dramatic.

That the donkey has contributed in any way, however slight, to the dedicated work carried out with these children shows once more how he continues to play his humble but invaluable role in the life of man.

12. The Truth and Nothing but ...

UNUSUAL OCCURENCES take place in most communities and a donkey establishment can produce its reasonable quota of out-of-the-way events without any effort. Ass idiosyncrasies give rise to incidents fraught with drama, due to their curiosity, sense of fun, lackadaisical attitude when ill, their often stolid mien that tempts one to poke fun at them, and a peculiar tendency to attract unusual situations.

Our trap mare Alana had a great sense of fun; a typical example of this occurred one day when she was required for an outing. She usually walked up or stood still to be captured, but this day she decided to play 'hard to get' and for about five to ten minutes gave as good a display of paddock antics as ever was seen from an adult ass. It would have been useless to try to catch her then, but when she had duly impressed us all, the game was over and she was ready to be caught for work.

This same lady became the heroine of an unexpected

fracas while on a family blackberry picking expedition. Alana, having carried a trap-load of us cheerfully to our destination escorted by our own and neighbouring dogs, and followed by a car, which transported the rest of the family and the picnic impedimenta, ambled along the bohereen behind us as we picked the fruit, when suddenly two dogs started a fight just beside her. With young children in the trap it was imperative for me to hold Alana in case she should bolt in fright, and this prevented me from trying to separate the combatants. So, calling loudly, I tried to attract the attention of the others some distance away and, as the cries of the underdog grew fainter, my cries grew stronger but evoked no response until an ear-shattering bray from Alana brought the necessary attention to restore law and order all around. Whether it was sheer excitement or utter disdain at my puny vocal efforts that brought forth her trumpeting call is debatable, but we all agreed that in the crisis her conduct was exemplary, and she was duly rewarded at teatime.

Much practised and enjoyed by a gay mare of ours called Misto was the art of communication. Inclined to confidential utterances rather than public address, she often exchanged spirited chatter in private with us, her intimate friends, while refusing to make a sound when among a crowd of human or animal kind.

A talking donkey! A tall story says the sceptic, but I am content to answer with the comment made by

Professor J. Arthur Thompson on the subject of animal communication: 'A sound is often a word and a word is enough for the wise.' The diversity of sounds brought forth from Misto would, if ever translated by a Dr Dolittle, show an admirable vocabulary.

The strange story of our little eighteen-month-old filly Echo is a real instance of 'while there's life, there's hope'. One Friday in November I noticed her in a field with her head held slightly sideways and walking unsteadily. I called in the vet at once, who said she had no temperature and, after a thorough examination, no visible sign of injury such as a cut or bruise. However, she got steadily worse in the following days. Her tongue became paralysed and hung limply out of her mouth. Unable to drink or feed herself at all, she had to be nourished with milk, water, and glucose by a tube up her nose through her gullet into her stomach.

She was now incapable of standing alone and was propped up in a small, straw-filled stable in a sitting position with sacks of hay for softness, while straw in sacks lined the wall. Rugs were wrapped around her, a small portable heater kept the stable warm and with the aid of a shaded bulb burning all night we were able to keep frequent watch. We massaged her legs to help the circulation and every few hours she had to be lifted from one side to another, with occasional fruitless efforts to make her stand; meanwhile her tongue hung helplessly out and symptoms of pneumonia were in sight.

With the unfailing attention of our vet, she continued in this state, until one morning at 2 am, twelve
days from the commencement of her illness, to my
nearly unbelievable joy, she managed to make some
slight movement of her mouth enabling her to suck
up a small quantity of warm milk, water and glucose.
A big step forward!

Yet two very black days were to follow, at the end
of which I must admit I gave up hope and was prepared to have her put to sleep. On our vet's advice,
however, I let another night go by and the miracle
happened. The next morning she looked obviously
brighter and from then on recovery began.

After eleven more days of feeding her, lifting her
up, and encouraging her to rise unaided, her head
being protected in her struggles by the straw-lined
walls, she managed to get up without help.

During those days we fed her nuts pushed on to
her back teeth, which she was able to munch without
biting her tongue, still limp and paralysed, and each
day she stood up for a little longer. An amusing, though
pathetic, sight was her first effort to eat hay. We
would come into the stable and see her with a bunch
of hay in her mouth sticking out at the sides like cat's
whiskers which, as she was still unable to eat, she just
sat there holding, presumably enjoying the taste.

Anyway she made an almost complete recovery,
save that her head was held one degree sideways. Our
vet said it was a brain condition due to an injury, or
something else. We kept her stabled for the rest of the

winter with a newly weaned foal for company. No matter how bad a situation is, it's seldom that there isn't some humour with it and this case was no exception.

As Echo started to improve I was able to attend to many things, neglected while she was ill, so had not the time to coddle her as before. Although she was quite obviously recovering, I noticed that when I visited her she would lie back on her pillows and look pathetic, and I began to suspect that a little play-acting was taking place! The next time our vet called I was out, so was not surprised, though highly amused, when my husband told me that he had noticed the same thing. Being ill was unpleasant, but all the attention was very pleasant and just because herself was getting better was no reason for the attention to get less!

Surely standing between the shafts of a cart containing milk churns with a coat thrown over its head is one of the most unusual of unusual things that can happen to an ass? Some people might think so but not the owner of the ass and cart that I once came across in a country town. Having enquired the reason for such an occurrence, I was told that as it was the ass's first day in the cart he was frightened by the splashing milk, but now 'what he don't know don't bother him.' A happier system of control is now in practice, I am glad to relate.

An amusing incident that took place in my mother's Kerry cottage is a sharp warning to people who sleep in strange places. With overcrowded accommodation, a young bachelor guest was allotted the sitting-room settee and not being initiated into the hazards of the locality, left the French window open when he retired. A native ass taking his morning stroll wandered into the room as was his wont at times, saw what he thought was a succulent piece of hay or herbage lying over the edge of the settee and, taking a nibble, was nearly startled out of his existence when it arose with a scream and confronted him attached to a human face!

An ass with a nocturnal wanderlust was Napoleon, the pet of a family whose house, together with their cook who was stone deaf, my widowed mother-in-law once rented. Awakened one night from her sleep by a terrific din in the room beneath her, she bravely sallied forth to investigate. Guided by the noise of heavy blows and the deep breathing of exertion she reached the sitting-room, and great was her relief when switching on the light she found not men in mortal combat but Napoleon engaged in a series of frantic acrobatic feats endeavouring to maintain a foothold on the highly polished parquet floor.

This same ass, a great music lover, was captivated by the piano, and would listen to it for hours resting his chin on the sill of an open window or stretched out on the lavender bed beneath.

Now to the ass as a collector's piece. My sister, when she was a child, decided that, as other members of the family had hobbies, she would have one too, and what better than collecting asses. This she proceeded to do from the neighbouring fields. As the collection of asses increased in our fields so likewise did the collection of questioning neighbours appear at our door—until a change of hobbies was enforced by our distracted parents.

One of the most curious mishaps to overtake a little ass was to be attacked by an otter. According to a farming acquaintance this fate befell a young foal of his while nibbling grass near the edge of a stream. An otter seized it by the leg and bit it so severely that it crushed the bones irreparably. My informant added that, as an otter will not relinquish his hold on a victim until he feels or hears a sharp crack or crunch, otter hunters known to him fill their boots with cinders to delude the otter. What a pity that these two delightful animals could not have been friends!

It is not pleasant to tell tales so it is with reluctance that I admit to having experienced two natural bad habits in the donkey. One of these was mentioned by John Mortimer as early as 1707 in *The Whole Art of Husbandry* in which the author says that the great impediment to keeping them is that they do injuries to trees. This is certainly true, and it is necessary to put a guard around valued trees, or put some creosote on the parts they can reach to prevent them biting off the bark.

Occasionally one comes across a donkey with the other bad habit that leads him in these parts to be called a 'thief', signifying an animal that quickly gets bored in a field and breaks out of it. This it does by lifting the latch of a gate with its mouth and guiding the bolt sideways until it opens, just as easily as we can do it with our hands, or jumping out, as the donkey can be a 'great lepper' when it is convenient to him. Equally effective ways of exit are to lie on the belly and wriggle through the wire, clamber over a bank or break through a fence. A mare we had called Betty Peg could have competed happily with Houdini. All donkeys enjoy a change of field and it is beneficial to them, but a natural 'thief' is quite a problem.

This unexpected agility is also remarkable in their play. Two yearlings of ours, a colt and a gelding who when not eating never ceased their cavorting around, displayed some nimble action in a game of 'trip you up first, sir'. The exhibitions of thrust and parry were both cunning and quick-moving. A mare, already the mother of two offspring, was very often the leader of the foals in their evening games and careered around in a very sprightly, though somewhat inelegant, manner with the youngsters, to the astonishment of the more dignified matrons.

Yes, our present-day donkey can be far from the inanimate object so often pictured in the mind's eye. He is a living creature, which in his animal way will reflect the personality of his owner and will repay with interest the treatment meted out to him. He is quick to recognize understanding in people, like Eeyore in *Winnie-the-Pooh*, who said to Christopher Robin: 'They don't think—that's what's the matter with so many of these others. They've no imagination. A tail isn't a tail to them, it's just a Little Bit Extra at the back.'

Betty Peg and Bruce, County Clare, 1962.

Top: The Twinnies Omi, a broken-coloured filly, and
Ome, the dark-brown colt to the right.
Above: The working donkey (Bill Doyle).

A yawning Paddy Medina with companion, Boghill,
Kilfenora, County Clare, 1985 (Jeannine Roman);
note the vestigial hoof.

Top: A group of Asiatic wild ass onagers in the Hai
Bar Wildlife Reserve, Israel (Itzhak Amit).
Above left: A grey donkey displaying its cross.
Above right: Our mule Firefly, sitting up like a dog,
Kilfenora, 1980.

Top: The author and her husband, Carol, presiding over a birthday party for the Twinnies, 9 July 1974. *Above:* Harry Cleeve coming to visit them on their twenty-fifth birthday, Thomastown, Kilkenny, 1996.

Top and above: The donkey as beast of burden, transporting milk (Bill Doyle) and hay in the west of Ireland.

Top: Kelpie being forcibly shod at Spanish Point Donkey
Stud, County Clare, 1968. *Above:* A rare combination
of horse, mule and donkey tilling the land in 1963

Top: John Simpson with donkey at Shrapnel Gulley,
Gallipoli, 1915 (Australian War Memorial).
Above: The Somali wild ass (William Ridgeway, *The
Origin and Influence of the Thoroughbred Horse*, 1905).

II

THE DONKEY IN THE WORLD

13. Derision

A MODERN WRITER on the ass faces the same difficulty as the Rev. J.P. Mahaffy foresaw in 1917 for anyone who 'set himself to explain how this animal, so dignified in early oriental history, should have been for centuries the emblem of stupidity and ridicule'. Mahaffy points out that it should be obvious to those who have made even the most superficial study of animals that the ass is no less intelligent than the horse, or other animals of higher pretensions either, while the jokes about him are at least as old as classical Greek. He goes on,

> This human idiosyncrasy has lasted to the present day. When permission was asked ten days ago by our secretary that I should read this paper, the proposal was received cordially, but with a burst of hilarity—a curious bit of evidence of how easy it is, with a topic worn threadbare through many centuries of repetition, to amuse even the higher varieties of the human species.

It is indeed the Greeks who appear to have started the idea that the ass was a stupid and, in their view, presumptuous creature, and so a subject of ridicule. The wild asses of Asia, having had such a reputation for being lively, handsome and fleet-footed, had degenerated into smaller, downtrodden-looking animals by the time they reached Europe, having intermingled and deteriorated en route. The Greeks, who had heard their praises sung through the ages, and who would have been told many stories of the part asses played in high places over previous centuries in countries both south and east of Greece, looked upon the woebegone creatures and assumed that they had appropriated to themselves those ancient glories out of vain presumption and derided them accordingly.

The esteem in which they were formerly held can be seen from the Standard of Ur, which came to light in recent times at Ur of the Chaldees, the birth place of Abraham, and is now in the British Museum. This shows the high regard for the animals in ancient times when, apart from peacetime duties, they drew the battle chariots in times of war.

On the war panel of the Standard each chariot is depicted as being drawn by a team of asses and carrying two men, one being the driver and the other a warrior whose task was to fling light javelins. As the chariots advance over the battlefield the asses walk sedately at the beginning, but become more and more excited until they finally break into a gallop. As shown on the Standard, the asses are driven in a headstall without a bit; but a nose ring is used when they are led.

In the army of Xerxes, the Indians, so Herodotus tells us, drove in chariots drawn by wild asses. It is an interesting fact that in India the ass never was, and still is not, a particular object of ridicule, perhaps for the simple reason that their eastern domesticated varieties of the asinine family, though smaller, are generally lively and swift-footed as opposed to the slower, lazier beasts of the west, which seem without energy except of a sensual nature.

Because the Greeks in time derided them, so also did the Romans who took many of their customs from the Greeks and, even when Rome became a centre of Christianity, they did nothing to deliver them from persecution, in spite of the ass's part in carrying Christ on Palm Sunday and other Christian associations.

Robert Graves has two explanations for this situation, which he gives in the introduction to his translation of *The Golden Ass* by Lucius Apuleius: in those far-off days the animal was sacred to the Egyptian god Set, known to the Greeks as Typhon, persecutor of the Egyptian goddess Isis and the murderer of her husband Osiris. The ass, therefore, typified lust, cruelty, and wickedness and there was a certain Egyptian festival (recorded by Plutarch) in which both asses and men of Typhonic colouring (sandy-red like a wild ass's coat) were pushed over cliffs in vengeance for Osiris's murder. 'Yet originally,' the author continues, 'the ass had been so holy a beast that its ears, conventionalized as twin feathers sprouting from the head of a sceptre, became the mark of sovereignty in the hand of every Egyptian deity.'

He also mentions their association in Europe with the winter Saturnalia at the end of which, he says, the ass-eared god was killed by his rival, a tradition that later developed into a Christmas fool wearing an ass-eared cap being killed by the spirit of the New Year. This explains the popular connection between an ass and a fool.

Professor Frederick Zeuner expresses his view that by comparison with the horse and the mule the ass is inferior, though he does not state a reason, and that its patience gave it the semblance of a slave. He considers that those influences, combined with the fact that in civilized countries it became the beast of the poor, have contributed to its low position in the social scale of domestic animals. Though the primary function of the ass was as a beast of burden, it was originally not despised. He continues that many races valued the animal and 'some Romans, too, appreciated the beauty of the well-bred asses'. In 260 BCE the Roman consul Cornelius Scipio Asina was given the name of Asina because of his large ears and retained it as his family name. So, one may deduce that in Rome in those days the ass was not derided.

Homer too, though very much earlier, appears to credit even a stubborn ass with good sense when he writes in the *Iliad*, 'Book XI':

As near a field of corn, a stubborn ass
O'er pow'rs his boyish guides and entering in,
On the rich forage grazes; while the boys
Their cudgels ply, but vain their puny strength,
Yet drive him out, when fully fed, with ease.

Yet Greeks and Romans in general did nothing to encourage in the ass that passion and spirited struggle for life that characterizes most animals. Having in time become ridiculous in the popular view, few people considered his noble qualities, and his decline in public esteem brought about a lack of care for his condition or circumstances, which in time led to actual physical decadence.

14. *Some Scattered Relations*

Having through long familiarity adjusted ourselves to the notion that an ass is an ass—and nothing more, it is surprising to encounter some of our donkey's distant, and not so distant, relations and their varied occupations.

By far the most distant is *Equus asinus hydruntinus*, a large name given to a small wild ass, which according to Professor Zeuner became extinct long before domestication began. It inhabited southern Europe, particularly Italy, and existed in similar form in Palestine and Jordan. He continues that in the late Pleistocene era (about 150,000 years ago) they had spread to south-western Europe, even to England and Germany which, he says, 'disposes of the many much-disputed fossils variously described as small *Equus caballus* or as *Equus asinus* or, most frequently, as *Equus hemionus*.'

The Irish Naturalists' Journal of 1925–7 says, 'Ass (E.a.) remains of a fossil ass are said to have been found in alluvial and cave deposits of the Pleistocene Age. But Professor Boyd Dawkins attributes its introduction as a domestic animal to the ninth century.'

I deliberately omitted mention of this ass from Chapter One to avoid confusion, because it became extinct so long ago and we know so little about it. Without any description of this animal, it is doubly tantalizing to know that it was possibly identical to the extinct North African wild ass.

Dealing with something less remote than fossils, we learn from Darwin that in Syria there used to be four distinct breeds: 'First a light and graceful animal, with an agreeable gait, used by ladies; secondly, an Arab breed reserved exclusively for the saddle; thirdly, a stout animal used for ploughing and various purposes; and lastly, the large Damascus breed, with a peculiarly long body and ears.' Incidentally the translation for Damascus in cuneiform writing is 'town of the asses'.

The same writer, quoting various sources such as Captain Marryat and Mr Blyth, gives an account of asses that were imported into Kentucky from Europe for the purpose of breeding mules. These, he says, seldom averaged more than fourteen hands, but the Kentuckians with great care managed to raise them to fifteen, and sometimes even to sixteen hands. The prices paid for those magnificent asses prove how much they were in demand, one notable stallion actually being sold for upwards of £1000. They were customarily exhibited at cattle shows, where one day was given over entirely to them.

In Missouri and New Orleans these large asses were also greatly prized, the reason being that the nature of the climate was particularly trying for horses. The chief source of these imported animals appears to have been Spain, and in the eighteenth century the asses there were described as being the best in Europe, on account of the climate and the care that was taken of them. There a 'large stout he-ass' frequently fetched 60 guineas while, if it was suspected that it was to be carried out of the country, 100 guineas was the price, although in Cordova in 1860 there is a record of £200 being paid for a stallion ass.

Of the Spanish asses the Catalonian had the reputation of being the finest. These were a good black, with white and mealy points, and a fine style of action. The Andalusian was similar, with a little more weight and bone, but these animals were all off-colours.

From there we look to Majorca, where the imported jacks were the heaviest in weight, bone, head and ears, but lacked style, finish and action. They were also said to reach sixteen hands, and were the largest of the European asses with the exception of the French Poitou. Although they were thought to have sprung originally from Spanish stock, the difference in structure and character had become marked, even the loud, sonorous voice being quite different from that of other breeds. The Poitou was specifically a brown ass and was altogether quite distinctive, even from the animals bred in Auvergne. But they had in common very careful owners because the fact that they flourished so well in that cold climate and gained such repute is undoubtedly due to the care they received.

Maltese asses were occasionally imported into America, but they were smaller than the Catalonian, although refined and thoroughbred in appearance. The Italian asses were the smallest of all.

In comparatively recent years some of our *asinus* relations from South Africa have been the subject of a sad story. After a season of ploughing they were generally sold for 10s. until, in 1950, their value rose considerably on the inauguration of a new business that was started near Natal. Here these animals were fattened, slaughtered and processed to obtain bone-meal, gelatine, hides and hair for felt manufacture, as well as red meat for salami, this latter finding a ready market in Germany and Italy and being exported in a deep frozen state. As the demand grew and was satisfied, the donkey population naturally declined; as it lessened the price rose, till at last the donkeys almost disappeared from the veld and the business failed.

Nearer home in the picturesque town of Clovelly in Devon the donkeys were still doing essential work in the late twentieth century on a cobbled street that wheeled traffic was unable to negotiate. Halfway down this street, which runs for about a mile down to the sea 500 feet below, is an inn which, although called the New Inn, is several hundred years old. All supplies arriving at the top of the hill for the hotel, as well as the luggage of its guests, were slid down to their destination on sledges. Everything to be brought up the hill was carried in wooden crates by donkeys.

The donkey's hooves, unlike those of a horse, are long, being concave beneath, with extremely sharp rims, and are admirably adapted for treading with security on slippery and rough surfaces. This place has the remnants of a very strong donkey force, as not so many years ago they transported coal from Wales, lime and fish, especially herrings, from the harbour to the rest of the village, which was on a slope.

A single ass that gave essential service for no less than half a century drew up the water from the great well at Carisbrook Castle in the Isle of Wight. At what age this animal commenced work is not known, but Brettel says, 'For the space of fifty years it worked daily at the wheel and, even then, died in perfect health and strength by accidentally falling over the ramparts of the castle.'

Centuries ago in Persia asses were taught the ambling gait that, along with the slitting of their nostrils to give them more wind, enables them to travel at such a rate that a horse must gallop to keep up with them. This is accomplished by the method of tying the fore and hind legs of the same side together with cotton lines at a greater or lesser distance apart, according to the step that the animal is desired to make. These lines are then fastened to the girth at the place of the stirrup and they are ridden thus by a groom every morning and evening until they become habituated to the pace.

There are still many donkeys in modern Iran including some small grey ones noted for their high turn of speed, but all of them, whether fast or slow, wear one or more bright blue ceramic beads as a protection against misfortune. These beads strung as necklaces are now greatly favoured by the tourists.

The grey smooth-coated donkeys of Kenya are sometimes to be seen in small herds because their owners don't care to part with them, especially the mares, and the males are never gelded. Up-country they are used for pulling carts with barrels of water. The carts have one long pole down the middle like the old South African cattle carts.

In times gone by one of the tribal hunting methods was to use them as stalking-horses. Disguised as antelope by means of painted marks, a mask over their head, and mock horns, they were driven towards the game, enabling the hunters concealed behind them to approach within bowshot.

Instances of the ass as a sacrificial offering are rare. The only one known to me is the sacrifice of large war asses by the Karmanians (in Persia) to their war god, Ares.

The best-known relative of the ass is the mule. It is no longer sought after in Ireland, although there are places where their services are still valued. I myself

have encountered them from time to time, indeed I
once owned one, but I know relatively little about
them. The following are some random notes written
upwards of two hundred years ago by men who in
their day observed them:

> The predilection which the Spaniards have long had
> for mules, has not only led them to prohibit all
> exports of she-asses but has lessened their regard for
> horses, so that the studs in Andalusia, formerly
> regarded as the best in Europe, have lost their credit,
> and 'future ages will hardly believe what has been
> truly said of the Spanish horses'.
>
> Mules do not breed, at least in temperate cli-
> mates, though some say that they do breed in hot
> countries. M. de Buffon the French naturalist (quot-
> ing Aristotle's *History of Animals*, Book VI, Chap.
> XXIV) states that the ancients positively assert that
> the mule can procreate with a mare (I presume a
> mule mare) at the age of seven years. And that a
> mule mare is capable of conception, though it never
> brings its fruit to maturity.
>
> Horse mares which have been covered by an ass
> go a whole year, and they cannot suckle their young
> above six months, on account of a pain in their teats.
>
> Mules should not be suffered to couple, because
> it makes them vicious and spiteful.
>
> At three months their legs have attained full
> growth, and double that length will be the height of
> the mule when full grown.

And now to a man whose observations made him
determined never to own a mule unless compelled to
do so by law, Josh Billings, the American humorist of

Civil War times. In *Essa on the Muel* he makes the following comments on this hybrid: 'The mule is haf hoss and haf Jackass and then kums to a full stop, natur diskovering her mistake. Tha are a modern invenshun, i dont think the Bible deludes tu then at all.' According to him, they can be trusted with anyone whose life is not worth more than their own. The only way to keep them in a pasture is to turn them into an adjoining field and let them jump out. He had known them, like some men corrupt at heart, to be good mules for six months just to get a good chance to kick somebody.

Mules were much used in some American states for pulling barges along the canals like the English barge horse, and in his inimitable way Billings gives the following account of one so used:

> Tha are the strongest creature on earth, and heaviest ackording tu their sise; I heard tell ov one who fell oph from the tow path, on the Eri kanawl, and sunk as soon as he touched bottom, but he kept on towing the boat tu the next stashun, breathing thru his ears, which stuck out ov the water.

15. Amongst Our Writers

IRISH AUTHORS HAVE NOT overlooked the donkey. James Stephens is among those who have written some delightful passages on our ass and his environment. People interested in donkey literature must, I feel, enjoy his writings about them.

In his book *The Demi-Gods*, the Mac Cann family and the angels were accompanied throughout their entire journey by an ass, whose participation in their activities, together with his own actions and thoughts, can be read again and again with sheer delight. In the first chapter one is highly entertained by Patsy Mac Cann and his daughter Mary who air their opinions over kissing an ass on the snout. Says Patsy, 'It's this way, that I don't like to see a woman kissing an ass on the snout, it's not natural or proper.' Replies Mary, 'A lot you know about natural and proper. Let you leave me alone now; and, besides that, doesn't the ass like it?' This argument on the merits or otherwise of kissing the ass's snout continues again in the last chapter until Patsy, thoroughly disgruntled by the whole matter, shouts, 'Will you leave that ass alone, Mary? Give him back his snout and behave yourself like a Christian girl.'

On another occasion the ass 'roared Hee-haw in a voice of such sudden mightyness, that not alone did the sleepers bound from their slumbers, but the very sun itself leaped across the horizon'. Travelling along the road he joins in their conversation, though silently, for 'he listened with such evident intention that no one could say he was out of the conversation'. He soliloquizes as the rain cascades over him. 'I'm very wet,' said the ass to himself, 'and I wish I wasn't.' And again, 'I don't care whether it stops raining or not, for I can't be any wetter than I am, however it goes.' He then dismisses the weather and settles himself to think about all the nice things to eat, concluding with oats, which he maintains are not a food but a blessing. Then shaking himself, he dissipates his thoughts.

In *The Crock of Gold* by the same author, an ass belonging to some travellers again figures. This one ate his fill at evening time and then lay down under a wall:

> He lay for a long time looking in one direction, and at last he put his head down and went to sleep. While he was sleeping he kept one ear up and the other one down for about twenty minutes, and then he put the first ear down and the other one up, and he kept doing this all night. If he had anything to

lose you wouldn't mind him setting up sentries, but he hadn't a thing in the world except his skin and bones, and no one would be bothered stealing them.

Nevertheless, there were people who bothered, for Lady Chatterton relates the story of a stolen ass in her *Rambles in the South of Ireland*. A gentleman was once walking across a common when he saw two Irishmen approaching, one of whom led a small donkey. On their passing a cottage an old woman rushed out and started to abuse them as thieves and robbers for carrying off her donkey.

The men replied that they had bought the animal that morning and continued to assert this in the face of a crowd that rapidly collected. Eventually someone remarked that the ass was said to know its owner and the ox his master's crib, and that the best thing to do was to let the creature herself decide. All parties agreed and the crowd moved away, leaving the ass by herself, whereupon she pricked up her ears, looked about her and marched off, taking the road diametrically opposed to the old woman's cottage. The old shrew vented her rage and disappointment on the two harassed men in a volley of epithets until, one of them stopped short and replied, 'You've given us throuble and vexation enough to rise the spirit out of any man. —I've two pounds in my pocket here, and by my sowl, I'll WEAR 'EM on you, aye, I will to the last penny, until I get my revenge.'

In *Spanish Lily* by K.F. Purdon the human element

is thoroughly dishonoured for the sufferings that are caused to the patient animals. This book was written in 1921 and in many ways the human attitude does not seem to have improved much in the intervening years, for the little beast of burden is often just as harshly used.

In the nineteenth century, however, Mary John Knott makes observations of a different kind. In her book *Two Months at Kilkee*, which was published in 1836, the author finds some of the donkeys in Clare not only remarkably pretty, but 'round, plump and very clean'. She goes on to comment on their gentleness, which is such that they pass quietly along without any bridle, carrying their panniers, with frequently a small child or two sitting behind without the least fear. She wonders if this is due to 'the sea-weed on which some of them choose to feed, or the boiled potatoes that are given to them when young', but in any case, she says, they do much credit to their owners.

It is Seamus MacManus who introduces the touch of fun, which is so often connected with the donkey in Ireland, by the story from Derry that he tells in *Through the Turf Smoke*. It appears that a certain farmer from Cruckagar in days gone by purchased an ass at a fair in the town and consulted with a friend, now a Derry merchant, but an erstwhile inhabitant of his own native village, as to how to get the animal home. Eventually it was decided to send him on the coach, as there happened to be no other passengers for Cruckagar on that particular day.

No sooner had the coach departed than the merchant, a merry fellow, dispatched a messenger to Cruckagar announcing that the Governor of the Apprentice Boys and Worshipful Master of the Londonderry Glorious Memories of Bloody Fields LOL 99,942 would be arriving in due course and that a royal Donegal welcome would be in order. The announcement had its effect and 300 Orangemen turned out with fife and drum to greet the distinguished visitor—who after many eulogies and musical tributes, stuck his head through the door of the coach and replied to them all in a 'long, loud and most harrowingly unmelodious bray'!

The 'Long Ears' of Patricia Lynch was more fortunate than some; he not only had a happy home, but had the gift of bringing the children who were his friends out into the Irish countryside to the fringes of fairyland, where they may have heard the poetry of the wind and of the bogs and become acquainted with the people who live in the wild places—on the islands and in the mountains and at the edges of the wide plains.

On the Aran Islands donkeys are particularly numerous owing to the rocky nature of the terrain, and two writers have something to say about their experiences with them there: Thomas H. Mason in *The Islands of Ireland* expresses surprise at the great number of them that are employed in drawing seaweed and turf and on Inishmaan he was unable to sleep a wink owing to the racket caused by dogs barking and asses galloping along the roads. He discovered that it was the time of year when the asses were free on the sand hills and during the night they would quietly approach the gardens around the cottages where the cabbages were grown. With great stealth the ass would push off a loose stone from the top of the wall with his nose and if there were no response from the dogs, would proceed to lower it until he could step into the garden and demolish the vegetables. Remarking to his hostess that he had no idea that asses could travel so fast as the sounds indicated, he was informed that they travelled best at night because: 'When the Holy Family were on the flight into Egypt they travelled with the ass by night and rested during the day, and ever since the ass travels best at night.'

Ian Dall in *Here are Stones* says that he was never before on an island where 'so many donkeys were to be found living as neighbours and with a certain amount of freedom to develop their characteristics'. He happened to answer the call of a cuckoo, also on Inishmaan, which he quickly altered to a bray when confronted by a donkey that rose and looked at him over the top of a wall, and was greatly interested when the animal threw back its head and replied to the challenge—'All the more so when from fields near at hand and places out of sight came a dozen answers.' He observes that everyone knows how a crowing cock is answered by every cock within earshot and that a child can set a village crowing, but he had not realized until that moment that donkeys also felt the contagion of that queer excitement!

An Irish ass—the wisest of beasts, proclaims Patrick Kavanagh in his book *The Green Fool*. A blessed animal, adds his friend, as they agreed that it was the ass that saved Patrick and his mother from the 'Wee Fellas' in fairyland when they got lost after an outing one wet and misty evening. Having traversed the country roads around Mullacrew with copious advice from wayside well-wishers, they were hopelessly lost. However, once they gave the ass his head, they very soon arrived home safe and sound, though a trifle damp. It is impossible not to be entertained by the details of their comic journey and indeed by every chapter of this absorbing book, which holds between its covers the quintessence of Irish rural life amongst the poorer people of his time, early in the 1900s.

Lady Clodagh Anson from her discreet memoirs, titled *Book*, published in 1931, writes about their donkey Torby who used to accompany them on their holidays to Ardmore, 'where he always got above himself and became very familiar'. Although relegated to outside quarters he preferred the house, and would open the back door with his teeth and be found asleep in front of the kitchen stove in the mornings. Later in the day, hee-hawing loudly, he would walk under the nursery window until the children dropped pieces of bread and jam into his mouth.

He followed his mistress around like a dog, escorting

her to the village, though stopping on the way to roll, and if she did not wait for him, would half sit up in the middle of his roll and bray requesting her, no doubt, to wait for him. When harnessed to his own little trap Torby would sally forth at breakneck speed scattering dogs, children and chickens in every direction.

A striking feature disclosed by these excerpts culled from the works of Irish writers is the affectionate and perceptive regard that the ass inspires in those who know him well; as for the others, the ass still makes his presence felt, irrespective of his surroundings and company, though often ill-used, undervalued and unappreciated.

16. In Verse

The Donkey

With monstrous head and sickening cry
And ears like errant wings,
The devil's walking parody
On all four-footed things.

In spite of these terrible afflictions ascribed so vividly to the donkey by G.K. Chesterton in his famous poem, he also recalls its day of days:

I keep my secret still.
Fools! For I also had my hour;
One far fierce hour and sweet:
There was a shout about my ears,
And palms about my feet.

This poem must by now have found a place on bookshelves the world over.

According to Kipling, however, if it weren't for Noah, the ass would never have had his hour of glory, because he had a great deal of trouble in getting him aboard the ark:

> Thin Noah spoke him fairly, thin talked to him
>   sevairely
> An' thin he cursed him squarely to the glory av the
>   Lord:
> Divil take the ass that bred you, an' the greater ass
>   that fed you!
> Divil go wid you, ye spalpeen'! an' the donkey wint
>   aboard.

So, without this efficacious curse, none of us would have ever seen a live donkey—any more than as Sam Weller says, 'There's another thing that no man never see and that's a dead donkey', and many of the world's writers and poets would have been lacking their inspiration.

Nor from *The Hills of Clare and Other Verses* by the poet of years gone by, Thomas Hayes, would have come Neddy, the rascal of a donkey who brought much happiness along with his liveliness on the mountain road from Kilmaley to Miltown Malbay.

Going to the Fair

> For the donkey, young and airy,
> Took some sudden wild vagary,
> And steep and crooked was the road, of all protection
>   bare,
> And the cart was toppling over,
> When her plight I did discover,
> And I saved that little cailin and she going to the fair

...
Though to her I was a stranger,
Now that she was out of danger,
She gratefully invited me to the 'pleasure board' to
    share,
And with Cupid for outrider,
Up I gladly sat beside her.
And we drove along right merrily to Miltown Malbay
    fair.

Patrick Kavanagh would have had to walk to the
fair without the aid of 'Kerr's Ass':

We borrowed the loan of Kerr's big ass
To go to Dundalk with butter,
Brought him home the evening before the market
An exile that night in Mucker.

The acquaintance of 'Doran's Ass' would have
been without a pleasant dream, as we can see from
the anonymous street ballad in Kathleen Hoagland's
A Thousand Years of Irish Poetry: Paddy Doyle was
courting Betty Toole and one night he took liquor and
fell asleep at the side of the road. When a big jackass
lay down beside him, Pat turned over and caressed
the animal happily until it began to bray. With that he
woke up and belted off in terror to Betty's door and
told her what had happened.

Says she—sure that was Doran's ass,
And so I believe it was says Pat.
They both got wed on the ensuing day,
But he never got back that new straw hat
That the jackass ate up on the way.

Perhaps the beautiful Miss Bradys would have been unable to attend 'Phil the Fluter's Ball'. Percy French might not even have issued the invitations:

> There was Mister Denis Dogherty who kep' The
> Runnin' Dog,
> There was little crooked Paddy from the Tiraloughett
> bog:
> There were boys from every Barony, and girls from
> every 'art',
> And the beautiful Miss Bradys, in a private ass an' cart.

Even the generosity of Padraic Colum's kind uncle would have proved unavailing.

Asses

> I know where I'd get
> An ass that would do,
> If I had the money—
> A pound or two.
> Said a ragged man
> To my uncle one day;
> He got the money
> And went on his way.
> And after that time,
> In market or fair,
> I'd look at the asses
> That might be there.
> And wonder what kind
> Of an ass would do
> For a ragged man,
> With a pound or two.

Peter Pindar, publishing his *Poetical Works* in

Dublin in 1791, would never have included the 'Ode
to my ass, Peter', an ode that shows an affection and
solicitude for his ass that will surprise many present-
day owners.

> Though, Balaam-like, I curs'd thee with a smack;
> Sturdy thou dropp'dst thine ears upon thy back,
> And trotting retrograde, with wriggling tail,
> In vain did I thy running rump assail.
> ...
> With such a smiling head, and laughing tail;
> And when I moved, HOW, griev'd thou seem'dst to say,
> 'Dear Master, let your humble ass prevail;
> Pray, Master, do not go away'—
> And HOW (for what friendship can be sweeter?)
> I gave thee grass again, O pleasant Peter.
>
> And HOW, when WINTER bade the herbage die,
> And Nature mourn'd beneath the stormy sky;
> When waving trees, surcharg'd with chilling rain,
> Dropp'd seeming tears upon the harass'd plain,
> I gave thee a good stable, warm as wool,
> With oats to grind, and hay to pull:
> Thus, whilst ABROAD DECEMBER rul'd the day,
> How PLENTY shew'd *within* the blooming May.

17. Donkeys and their Owners

THE DONKEY IS FORTUNATE, and we are fortunate, in that among the innumerable owners of this often ill-used creature have been poets and writers of many nationalities who have been able to share with us the enchantment that they have found in his company. It is an enchantment that anyone can seek, once its endless varieties have been revealed by these artists. Barriers of age or of profession are non-existent: the small child, the learned man, the painter or the wanderer can all partake of it, according to their ability.

As Federico Diaz-Falcon, writing about the donkey Caravaco, beloved of tourists in Majorca, says, 'Just as there are men with donkey's faces, so there are donkeys with men's faces.' He goes on to wonder whether 'wise men, Egyptologists and poets prefer donkeys because of their romantic tendencies'.

Into this category of Egyptologists comes Arthur Weigall, who at one time possessed a white Egyptian donkey that bore the name of Cicero. Cicero was big and handsome, and romantic with a vengeance. He not only brayed with shattering intensity whenever a lady donkey appeared on the horizon, but should some indiscreet tourist happen to be riding upon the object of his passion, this obstacle to love would very soon be forcibly removed and deposited in the sand while Cicero advanced his suit. Alas, on his owner's departure from Egypt this amorous beast was bought by a rich and elderly widow from France, who wanted him for pulling her about her estate in a kind of invalid chair. The unsuitability of her purchase became apparent all too soon, and the gallant lover ended his days as a eunuch.

If this was tragedy, it is offset by the donkey of the little Italian, Pepino, who was responsible for a miracle and is so charmingly described by Paul Gallico in his book *The Small Miracle*. This donkey, Violetta, was the sole possession of the orphan boy and they earned their living together as haulage contractors in Assisi. When Violetta fell sick, her master in his anxiety sought permission to take her into the crypt of St Francis, where he was sure a cure would be effected. The Supervisor refused, so Pepino went to Rome and asked the Pope himself to intervene. The Pope granted the wish of the little boy, and when the mason was clearing the passageway for the donkey to enter, an arch collapsed revealing the long-lost legacy of St Francis.

The way was then clear for the pair to pass through and as they disappeared from view, the donkey's hoof beats rang out briskly and the ghost of a smile flickered about her mouth.

Pepino was lucky in that he inherited Violetta: Padraic Ó Conaire, the wandering writer of Galway, had to buy his little black ass, and the hard way—from a traveller. Falling in love with him at the fair of Kinvara, he offered his owner £1 and the bargain was finally clinched at that—plus the payment of 6d. to each of the man's children. Needless to say that traveller suddenly became the most prolific man in the country with a brood that rivalled the Golden Horde, but when eventually all were appeased, the ass bore his new owner away to the woods at a gallop. They continued their peregrination (at an easier pace, of course) for many years and all who accompany them in retrospect along the byroads of Ireland will meet such people as they never knew existed and discover an undreamed of magic in field and fair.

Expeditions of a similar nature may be entered upon under the guidance of the Spanish poet, Juan Ramon Jimenez, and his donkey, Platero, in their native Andalusia. This gay, sophisticated little animal discovers for his rider (and for you who read about him) all the mysterious and the wondrous things that lie hidden in the twilight and under the golden blossoms and in the hearts of the inhabitants of Moguer. A journey with Platero, as with most poets, is a journey through an unknown world—which turns out in the end to be the same old everyday one that everybody, and no one, knew about.

The fair land of France, or a portion of it, is covered by Robert Louis Stevenson, whose baggage was carried somewhat unwillingly by Modestine, 'a diminutive she-ass, not much bigger than a dog, the colour of a mouse, with a kindly eye and a determined under jaw'. Modestine cost the writer 65 francs, a glass of brandy, a great deal of energy and many cries of 'Proot!' before she was finally goaded into motion. They travelled 120 miles together during twelve days, the donkey being sustained chiefly by black bread, and perhaps the greatest tribute to her race is the fact that Stevenson, in spite of the desperation that she frequently caused him to feel, wept uninhibited tears after he had sold her at the end of the trip.

Today, an annual tribute to their constant companion is also paid by the citizens of California, where prospectors from all over the area around Death Valley are invited to take part every year in a curious contest. Making the occasion their yearly trip to civilization, the competitors are required to light a fire, cook a pancake and feed it to their mokes, when the first one to finish wins a handsome prize for its master.

The Spaniards have a high regard for these animals too, but it is shown in, to our minds, a strange way. Gerald Brenan tells of an instance of this in his book *South from Granada*, which was published in 1958. He describes a young couple named Placido and Isabel, who had four or five children and a few strips of land, together with a donkey. Placido supplemented his peasant's earnings by collecting and selling brush-wood with the help of the donkey. One day the donkey fell and broke its leg, thus causing a financial crisis, as the family were too poor to buy another one.

Mr Brenan went along to see if he could help them over the calamity and he found the young wife nursing a baby and on the verge of tears. She proclaimed that there was nothing to be done except 'throw the donkey away', although it broke her heart as it had been brought up with the children. He discovered that 'throwing it away' consisted of pushing it down a precipitous slope into a ravine among other dead and dying animals, where it would lie until it died or the vultures finished it off. He expostulated that it must first be killed, but Isabel said that they could never do that as it would be far too cruel—that nobody in the village ever killed mules, donkeys or cows. In a predicament, Mr Brenan then approached the smith and offered him a sum of money to kill the animal, but the man refused on the grounds that the opinion of the village would be against him if he accepted, and so all that he could do was to try to persuade Placido to push the creature over a real precipice, where it would be instantly killed. Whether he carried this out, however, is doubtful as, in the words of the author, 'village customs had a way of imposing themselves'.

Another unlucky ass, but one that gave rise to a most amusing situation, belonged to a certain alder-man in the famous tale of *Don Quixote*. This man had lost his ass and was told by another alderman of the same town that he had lately seen it on the mountain. The two men went off together to seek the missing animal, but without success. Eventually the one who had seen it proposed that they should separate and bray at intervals, the assumption being that the missing ass would himself bray in reply. All that was achieved, however, by this manoeuvre was a mutual conviction on the part of each alderman that the other one was the animal that they sought! No reply was elicited from the missing one—which was not surprising in view of the fact that it had by that time been partly devoured by wolves, but it was commemorated, albeit in mockery, by the inhabitants of the neighbouring villages giving utterance to a bray whenever they encountered a fellow townsman of the two aldermen, this jest going so far that on occasion the mocked even sallied forth in arms against the mockers.

Life Magazine, in a beautifully illustrated article published in 1969 and titled 'The Marvels of Egypt's Past', referred to the ancient Egyptians' enjoyment of raillery and wisecrack, stating

> their jokes turned up in tomb paintings, like captions on modern cartoons. Among a group of donkey drivers resting in a field, one cried out, 'I've brought four pots of beer.' To which another cracked, 'That's nothing. I've loaded my donkey with 200 sacks while you were sitting on your backside.'

A flow of backchat with an astonishingly modern

flavour began centuries before Christ.

Rene Gardi, the French writer, in a story of a journey made by him across the Sahara, describes a sojourn by a well at El Golea, during which he was intrigued to observe an Arab at work manuring his garden. On the man's donkey, in use as sacks that were slung down each side of the animal's back to hold the dung, was the most beautifully-woven Berber cloth, which in Europe would certainly only be used for the best possible cushion covers and bedspreads.

In Sicily what goes on the donkey's back is less magnificent than what follows behind him, for there the donkey-carts were long decorated with elaborate carvings and gaily coloured in red, yellow, blue and green to symbolize the island's oranges, sun, sea and grass. Well made and well balanced, they flaunted scenes from French and Sicilian history, reflecting not only the temperament, taste and traditions of the people but the financial status of their owners. Through the ages it has been the ambition of even the poorest farmers and traders to possess one of these beautiful carts, known centuries before Christ in Sicily, but today's tourists are more likely to come across horse-drawn carts of this type.

To return to the donkey itself, it is astonishing what an ass can accomplish once it makes up its mind. In 1954 the weekly magazine called *Ireland's Own* published an article by D. O'Dee, an account of a donkey living at Gibraltar many years ago who was bought by a new owner in Malta and sent on its way there by sea. Unhappily the ship struck a sand bank off Cape de Gat and the ass was thrown overboard in the somewhat forlorn hope that it might make land, although the seas were running so high that a boat that left the ship was lost.

Nevertheless, a few days later the guard who opened the gates of Gibraltar in the morning was surprised to see the animal standing before him, and on being admitted, it made straight for the stable where it had previously lived. So, not only had it swum safely to shore, but had found its way over 200 miles of completely unknown territory, through mountainous country intercepted by streams, in such record time that it could not have mistaken the direction even once.

18. Folklore, Mythology and Tradition

AS MIGHT BE EXPECTED from its far-flung connections, the donkey turns up all over the world in folklore, mythology and tradition. For one thing, the cross on its back is considered to be a symbol of Christianity because Christ rode upon it, and there is an old Irish saying that the ass always kneels on Christmas night. A tradition from Mayo also holds that there is always a black spot on an ass's leg that was put there by Our Lady's thumb.

It is said, too, that St Anthony refused to believe in the presence of Christ in the Eucharist unless his ass left its stable and knelt before the Sacrament. A few days later, when St Anthony was leaving the church to carry the Eucharist to a dying man, the ass met him at the steps and knelt before the Sacrament. The saint is frequently portrayed in paintings with a kneeling ass.

Probably because of its association with the Holy Family, the Irish have always had great faith in the curative powers of the ass. Lady Chatterton in *Rambles in the South of Ireland* relates the story of a certain gentleman who had a contretemps with some workmen, who were repairing his house and who failed on one occasion to return from an errand with the donkey and cart. On going to investigate the cause of the delay, he discovered the animal outside the smith's forge surrounded by a crowd of women, who were engaged in passing a half-naked child round and round over its back. Answering his expostulations, one of the women replied that the child had fits and that they were curing him by passing him nine times nine under the donkey. The gentleman remarked that it would surely be much better to feed and clothe the child properly, but he was told indignantly that if that treatment didn't cure him, nothing else would.

Le Fanu, writing at the end of the nineteenth century, remarks on the curative powers of the animal and the subsequent regard in which it was held. In *Seventy Years of Irish Life* he says that he remembers how, early in that century, one Ned Sullivan supported himself and a large family by wandering throughout the country crying out: 'Will anyone come under my ass for the chin-cough?' Donkeys' milk was esteemed to such a degree among the richer people of the country that the superstition arose that donkeys had the power to cure whooping cough. The milk was also supposed to be good for consumptives, so he says, as it was less sugary and cheesy than cows' milk.

Lady Wilde affirms this belief of the Irish in the efficacy of the ass—or parts of it—as a charm in times of stress. In *Ancient Cures, Charms and Usages of Ireland* we read that the peasants have great faith in the scapular, which is worn round the neck as a talisman against all evil demons, fairies or witches. But if a woman is in great danger during a confinement, 'a strip of the skin of an ass, and a piece of the hoof are also tied around her neck in memory of the travail of the Holy Mother in the stable at Bethlehem.' If the woman is actually dying, however, the scapular must first be removed, 'for if she dies with it on, she carries away the blessing out of it and it has no more virtue until reblessed by the priest.'

One of the many stories in which lions and asses figure together is told in connection with St Jerome while he was living at his monastery in Bethlehem. One day a lion, limping grievously, suddenly appeared, causing the other monks to flee in terror. St Jerome however, in complete confidence, examined the lion's paw and removed from it a deeply embedded thorn. The lion, to show his gratitude, became the constant companion of the saint. But more trouble was in store for him. The other monks decided that the lion should work to earn his keep like everyone else, and so St Jerome ordered him to act as a guard for the ass of the convent on its trips to fetch wood. All went well until one day the lion wandered off into the desert, leaving the ass unguarded, when it was seized by robbers and sold to a caravan of merchants.

When the lion returned he could not, of course, find the ass and so had to go back to the convent alone and in great distress. The monks assumed that he had eaten the ass and ordered that he should do the work of the animal in atonement. The lion obeyed in perfect humility, but one day he recognized the ass in a passing caravan and triumphantly brought the whole company to the convent to prove his innocence.

Many festivals of the ass were celebrated in churches in the middle ages and, although these may sound ridiculous to modern notions, they were by no means intended as irreverent. On the contrary, they were to celebrate the ass for the various parts it played in biblical history.

In France in mediaeval times a famous, though strange, celebration was held at Beauvais on the fourteenth of January each year, which represented the Flight into Egypt. A richly caparisoned ass on which rode a young girl clasping a child or doll was escorted with much ceremony to the church, where the procession was received by the priests, who led the ass and its burden to the sanctuary. Mass was then sung, but instead of the usual responses the congregation chanted 'hin-ham', meaning 'hee-haw'. At the close of mass the priest turned to the people and, instead of *Deo gratias*, thrice responded 'hin-ham'.

An ass knows all, they say, because with his long ears he hears all, but King Midas had his ears changed into those of an ass as a sign of ignorance and stupidity. Midas attempted to conceal this indignity from his subjects, and a servant who saw the length of his ears and was afraid of not being able to keep the secret, opened a hole in the earth, whispered the information inside and covered it up. However, on that place a number of reeds grew up which, when agitated by the wind, uttered the secret words that had been buried beneath them.

Alas for Midas! But he was lucky that he was able to keep his own head, for Scot in his *Discoveries of Witchcraft*, published in 1584, gives a recipe for affixing an ass's head on a man.

Then there was Lucius Apuleius, born in Morocco early in the second century, who relates the marvellous tale of his own transformation into an ass because he tried to meddle in witchcraft. The Golden Ass can only return to human shape when he eats rose petals, but in the meantime he has all sorts of exotic and erotic adventures, which are greatly enhanced by the fact that he has retained his human understanding and desires.

The cure in ancient times for the sting of a scorpion was also a question of magic. The sufferer from this affliction was required to sit upon an ass with his face to the tail, or whisper in the animal's ear, 'A scorpion has stung me.' In either case apparently the pain was transferred from the man to the ass, but it was necessary that the ceremony should be performed on a lucky day and at a lucky hour.

In Morocco, the donkey's ear, or part of the ear, was regarded as having aphrodisiac powers. To be effective it must be placed in the food of the person in question, who must be unaware of taking it. My informant states

> Needless to say, one uses the ear of someone else's donkey. A very sharp knife is concealed in the hand, entering a crowded animals' 'fondak' [a kind of parking place] and pushing through the animals without stopping, an ear is grasped and removed with a single slash. This is the reason so many donkeys are minus all or part of an ear. It is now a punishable offence, but the ear collector is very quick and, I am told, makes good money.

There are many countries in the world where the ass figures in legend, folklore and tradition. Ireland has many stories; some of them relate to his cleverness and some of them poke fun at him—or use him as a means of poking fun at others.

As far back as the '98 Rebellion, for instance, as we are told by Dr Richard Hayes, the Anglo-Irish authorities had issued a wretched caricature of a French officer riding a miserable moke and singing a weird doggerel called 'Erin go Bray', a parody of *Erin go Bra*—Ireland forever.

The donkey's cleverness is illustrated by a legend from a village in County Mayo, recounted by John McCann in *Ireland's Own* in May 1955. An old lady there owned an ass whose only food during the week consisted of the grass that he could find along the roadsides of the locality. Sundays, however, were different and these were proclaimed to all and sundry, including the ass, by the ringing of the mass bell. The moment the little animal heard this sound he would proceed rapidly to the gates opening into the church grounds, where he knew there was a feast of fresh green grass, accessible only when the gates were open for mass. Eventually the cleverness of this creature became a byword and he was always allowed to partake of his Sunday dinner, his ingeniousness still being related many years later.

That it was possible to hypnotize the ass was found out by E.S. Dodgson from the Basques of both French and Spanish Navarre, who gave him the following details from the folklore of their region: 'if you knock a donkey down, bellow very loudly into its ear, and stop the ear before you end your braying with a large stone. The astonished quadruped will then lie in an apparent sleep for an hour or more.'

Irish asses are never hypnotized. It would be an insult to their perspicacity and might interfere with the things that they tell us. For instance, when an ass brays, don't we all know that another traveller's passed away? And, if you do not like a person, you would be well advised not to go within 'an ass's roar' of him, any more than if you are busy you would go near a person who is liable to 'talk the hind leg off a donkey'!

19. *The Ass in the Bible*

NO BOOK on the ass could be complete without reference to the Bible and a measure of the erstwhile importance of that animal is the number of times he is mentioned therein. Starting off with Genesis there is a description of one of the twelve tribes of Israel in 49:14 that reads: 'Issachar is a strong ass couching down between two burdens.' This bears a curious similitude to the way the Irish transport their turf, seaweed and other goods in the basket panniers.

In the days of its glory, however, its chief burdens were kings, as before the time of David it was considered improper for royalty to ride a horse rather than an ass, according to a text from the ancient city of Mari that existed on the banks of the Euphrates in the second and third millennium. Its finest hour is foretold in Zechariah 9:9, when the prophet says: 'Rejoice greatly, O daughter of Zion; shout, O daughter of Jerusalem: behold thy king cometh unto thee, he is just, and having salvation; lowly and riding upon an ass, and upon a colt, the foal of an ass,' the prophecy being, of course, fulfilled by Christ on Palm Sunday.

It is interesting to note that in early times there was a method of travel that may well have been familiar to Zechariah requiring two asses, side by side, to carry the traveller. He sat on a seat that was slung between them in a kind of double harness. From the song of Deborah and Barak, Judges 5:9–10, we learn the colour of these mounts on the elect: 'Bless ye the Lord. Speak, ye that ride on white asses, ye that sit in judgement, and walk by the way.' Pierre van Paassen in his studious book *Why Jesus Died* states: 'He rode on a white donkey as tradition demanded at the installation of a new monarch.' By this time the horse had become a symbol of war and Christ was not to come as a military leader, but to come in peace.

The prophets, indeed, found it convenient on more than one occasion to incorporate the ass in their predictions or to use it as a symbol. In I Samuel 9, it can be seen that asses played no small part in the story of Israel's appointment of her first king, Saul. Saul's father, a Benjamite chief named Kish, lost some asses and sent Saul and a servant to look for them. After a long search without finding them, Saul would have returned home, but the servant suggested that they should consult Samuel, a seer, now called a prophet. 'A man of God and he is an honourable man: and all that he saith cometh surely to pass.' Not only did

Samuel tell them that the asses were found, but having been prepared by God for this meeting, presented Saul to the people, who received him as their king.

It is interesting to note in the previous chapter that asses were among the material things the Lord told the Israelites that a king would demand from them. 'And he will take your asses and put them to his work' (I Samuel 8:16).

In Exodus and Isaiah the ass is not only mentioned with the ox in one of the commandments, but the prophet Isaiah laments somewhat cynically that though the ox and the ass find their way to their owner's house, God's chosen people, though treated with the kindliest care, show no such intelligence.

God himself even found occasion to speak through the mouth of an ass in what is perhaps the least comprehended of all ass stories. In Numbers 22:28, he expresses his disapproval of Balaam's self-will by causing his beast of burden to say, 'What have I done unto thee, that thou has smitten me these three times?' This is a parallel to the serpent in the Garden of Eden, Genesis 3, which is the only other mute creature recorded in the Old Testament as using human speech.

Are there not, after all, such things as miracles? And if there are, who better to perform them than the Almighty, he who has endowed animals with this extra sense enabling them frequently to disclose to us the unseen? God conveys his messages in many ways, so why not speak to Balaam through an ass? But I wonder how many million times over the ages the animal has repeated in its mind these particular words of God in desperation.

This same animal has been used many times in tales and myths to emphasize the wickedness of rebellion against God, usually in conjunction with a lion, and I feel that the Old Testament story in I Kings 13 must have been the forerunner of them. This describes a lion that killed a prophet who disobeyed the word of God, but did not touch the ass on which he was riding. The corpse was found by passing men with the lion and ass standing by—the lion not having touched the corpse or injured the ass.

Instructions regarding asses were also laid down by the prophets. Isaiah, for instance, insists in 30:24 that, 'The oxen likewise and the young asses that ear the ground shall eat clean provender, which hath been winnowed with the shovel and with the fan', and in Deuteronomy 22:10, it is stated, 'Thou shalt not plough with an ox and an ass together.'

Obviously their well-being was of some concern to these men, because apparently Job himself owned 1000 she-asses, they being more valuable for their milk and foals. No males are mentioned specifically, leaving it to the reader's imagination. The same prophet in 11:12 states categorically: 'For vain man would be wise, though man be born like a wild ass's colt,' and in 1:14, the touch of absolute peace before Satan struck the first blow against him is conveyed by the description of a scene where, 'The oxen were ploughing and the asses were feeding beside them.'

In ordinary times these highly regarded animals were certainly not eaten, but in a time of crisis they became particularly valuable, as can be deduced from II Kings 6:25. This is an account of the siege of Samaria, which took place in the time of Elisha, and of the ensuing famine during which an ass's head was sold for the large sum of fourscore pieces of silver.

They figure in another famine, too. Jeremiah describes in 14:6 how, 'The wild asses stand in high places. They snuffed up the wind like dragons and their eyes did fail because there was no grass.' But this snuffing also conveys another picture, and earlier on in 2:24, Jeremiah has described an ass in her season:

A wild ass used to the wilderness, that snuffeth up the wind in her desire; in her occasion who can turn her away? all they that seek her will not weary themselves; in her month they shall find her.

In the hymn to creation they had their place as well, for in that loveliest of Psalms, the 104th (10–12), is the verse,

He sendeth the springs into the rivers which run
    among the hills.
All beasts of the fields drink thereof: and wild asses
    quench their thirst.
Beside them shall the fowls of the air have their
    habitation and sing among the branches.

Nor are they left out of Proverbs. In 26:3, it is said,

'A whip for the horse, a bridle for the ass and a rod for the fool's back.'

In Bible times there were the wild asses that lived in herds away from human habitation and were easily scared, as well as the domesticated ass mostly used for human transport and which was, as previously stated, the recognized animal for carrying the great.

The Hebrew words for the latter are rendered *aton*, which refers to its endurance, and *hamor*, from the reddish coat of the most usual colour form. There were also two words used to describe the wild ass—*arod* and *pere*. *Pere* is recognized today as referring to the onager, which is still to be found in parts of western and central Asia. In recent years a large island in the Aral Sea called Barsa-Kelmes was colonized with onager, of which there are now fifty head on the island. They are also to be found in large herds on an island in the sea of Azov, in the southern Ukraine. Until 1920 there were wild asses in Jordan.

Today animals have their own special prayers, for on Horsemen's Sunday, which has been celebrated on Epsom Downs on the last Sunday in September for more than fifty years, a service is held for horses, ponies and donkeys. As these services are now held in many places throughout the world, it is perhaps a sign of growing recognition that, next to man, animals are justly entitled to our tenderness, respect and consideration in return for the essential benefits that we receive from them.

When we remember that once our Lord had need

of the ass, it ought to have been one of the first animals to be thus recognized and not one of the last.

We should bear in mind, when losing any beloved
pet, that as our Lord created them, we must entrust
them to his loving care as someday we must entrust
ourselves. In the meantime let me end with our Lord's
own words, on sending the disciples to collect the ass
and her colt, for his entry into Jerusalem on Palm
Sunday: 'And if any man say aught unto you, ye shall
say the Lord hath need of them' (Matthew 21:3).

20. An Honorary Member

LTHOUGH NOT AN Irish donkey, there was an offspring of this equine family that many a race would be proud to adopt as an honorary member. This was the legendary donkey of the 1915–16 Gallipoli Campaign.

Observed feeding in a gully the day after the Anzacs landed on the peninsula, the donkey was annexed by Private John Simpson Kirkpatrick, a stretcher-bearer of Anglo-Scottish descent, who enlisted in Western Australia in 1914 as John Simpson.

Simpson was a man with an inborn love and understanding of animals, so it was not surprising that when he came across a small bewildered donkey, they struck up a companionship in this frightening and unknown world. Very soon Simpson realized the value of such a companion in his work. The story of how for three weeks they went up and down Shrapnel Gully together under constant bombardment, bringing wounded soldiers back to the casualty base, is not only a legend in Australia, where a bronze statue to the memory of 'The Man with the Donkey' is erected at the Shrine of Remembrance in Melbourne, but it is surely one of the finest stories of human and animal co-operation to come out of any war.

Known as the 'Bravest of the Brave' by fellow soldiers, Simpson cheerfully went about his rescue work whistling and talking to his donkey (as was verified by his comrades), the animal often wearing a Red Cross armlet around his head. He called it a diversity of names according to his mood, sometimes Abdul, occasionally Murphy, but mostly Duffy; though Queen Elizabeth—after the great battleship—got a turn too!

At last, as once again they were on the way down to the base, an enemy bullet put an end to their combined work of mercy. With a shot through his brave heart, Simpson fell beside the donkey, who, it is said, returned alone to the casualty base with his burden.

Little is known of where this tiny donkey came from, but a possible explanation is that it was one of two that were known to have been brought to test the drinking water, as it was well known that donkeys will not drink impure or poisoned water. This once again confirms the delicacy of their drinking habits.

Where he ended his days is also a matter of conjecture, but he is certainly not forgotten. On the eightieth anniversary of the Gallipoli campaign the donkey was posthumously awarded the Purple Cross—created by the RSPCA to recognize the efforts

and service of animals in war—by Australia's Deputy Prime Minister, Tim Fischer. And, as I have personally witnessed on visits to the peninsula, many visitors ask to see the grave of the man with the donkey.

A detailed account of 'this fascinating story of an ordinary man who did extraordinary things in a critical situation' is to be found in a book of absorbing research by Sir Irving Benson called *The Man with the Donkey*, published in 1965.

Assuredly he can be welcomed in memory as an honorary member by all Irish donkeys.

Select Bibliography

Anson, Lady Clodagh, *Book* (London 1931).

Benson, Sir Irving, *The Man with the Donkey* (London 1965).

Berry, Christine, and Kokas, Jo-anne, *Donkey Business III* (The Good Samaritan Donkey Sanctuary, New South Wales, 1998).

Brenan, Gerald, *South from Granada* (London 1958).

Chatterton, Lady, *Rambles in the South of Ireland, during the year 1839* (London 1839).

Chesterton, G.K., *Stories, Essays and Poems* (London 1965).

Cornish, C.J., *Life at the Zoo* (London 1895).

Dall, Ian, *Here are Stones* (London 1931).

Diaz-Falcon, Federico, *All Donkeys are Ready*, trans. Alan Turner (Palma de Mallorca 1961).

Dillon, Myles, 'The Book of Adam and Eve in Ireland', *Celtica*, IV (1958), 37.

Dutton, Hely, *Statistical Survey of County Clare* (Dublin 1808).

Evans, E. Estyn, *Irish Heritage* (Dundalk 1949).

Fitzpatrick, W.J., *The Life, Times & Contemporaries of Lord Cloncurry* (Dublin 1855).

French, Percy, *Prose, Poems & Parodies* (Dublin 1964).

Gallico, Paul, *The Small Miracle* (London 1963).

Gardi, Rene, *Blue Veils, Red Tents* (London 1950).

Googe, Barnaby, *Foure Bookes of Husbandrie* (London 1577/1586).

Greenwood, James, *Wild Sports of the World* (London 1862).

Herodotus, *The Histories* (Harmondsworth, Middlesex 1954).

Hoagland, Kathleen, *A Thousand Years of Irish Poetry* (New York 1947).

Holinshed, Raphael, *Chronicles* (London 1577/1586).

Jiminez, Juan Ramon, *Platero and I* (Oxford 1957).

Joyce, P.W., *A Social History of Ancient Ireland* (London 1903).

Kavanagh, Patrick, *The Green Fool* (London 1938).

—, 'Kerr's Ass' in *Collected Poems* (London 1964).

Kelly, Professor Fergus, *Early Irish Farming: A Study Based Mainly on the Law-Texts of the Seventh and Eigth Centuries A.D.* (Dublin 1997).

K'eogh, John, *Zoologia Medicinalis Hibernica, or a Treatise of Birds, Beasts, Fishes, Reptiles or Insects, which are commonly known and propagated in this Kingdom. Giving an account of their Medicinal virtues and names in English, Irish and Latin* (Dublin 1739).

Knott, Mary John, *Two Months at Kilkee* (Dublin 1836).

Le Fanu, W.R., *Seventy Years of Irish Life* (London 1899).

Lydon, James F., *The Irish Sword*, 5/21 (Winter 1962).

MacManus, Seamus, *Through the Turf Smoke* (New York 1899).

Mahaffy, Rev J.P., Provost of Trinity College Dublin, 'On the introduction of the ass as a beast of burden into Ireland', *Proceedings of the Royal Irish Academy* XXXIII/17 and 18 (March 1917), Section C.

Mason, Thomas H., *The Islands of Ireland* (Cork 1967).

Maxwell, Constantia, *Dublin under the Georges* (London 1956).

Maxwell, W.H., *Wild Sports of the West* (London 1832).

Mills, John, *A Treatise on Cattle* (Dublin 1776).

Moore, George, *Hail and Farewell* (London 1912).

Mortimer, John, *The Whole Art of Husbandry, or, The Way of Managing and Improving of Land* (London 1707).

Morton, H.V., *In Search of Ireland*, 9th edn (London 1934).

Pindar, Peter, *The Poetical Works of Peter Pindar* (Dublin 1791).

Purdon, K.F., *Spanish Lily* (Dublin 1921).

Ridgeway, William, *Origin and Influence of the Thoroughbred Horse* (Cambridge 1905).

Rutty, John, *An Essay Towards the Natural History*

   of the County of Dublin (Dublin 1772).

Stephens, James, *The Crock of Gold* (London 1965).

—, *The Demi-Gods* (London 1926).

Stevenson, Robert Louis, *Travels with a Donkey* (London 1925).

Tegetmeier, W.B. and C.L. Sutherland, *Horses, Asses, Zebras, Mules and Mule Breeding* (London 1895).

van Paassen, Pierre, *Why Jesus Died* (New York 1949).

Walsh, Maurice, *The Road to Nowhere* (London 1935).

Weigall, Arthur, *Laura was my Camel* (New York 1932).

Zeuner, Frederick, *History of Domesticated Animals* (London 1963).

Index